THE
DEEPER
INTELLIGENCE

THE DEEPER INTELLIGENCE

ANDREW M. HODGES, M.D.

TRANSIT

Published in Nashville, Tennessee, by Thomas Nelson, Inc.

The names of persons and certain details of case histories described in this book have been changed to protect the author's patients. In some cases composite case histories have been constructed from actual cases.

Library of Congress Cataloging-in-Publication Data

Hodges, Andrew G.
    The deeper intelligence / Andrew G. Hodges.
        p.   cm.
    Includes bibliographical references.
    ISBN 0-7852-0089-4
    1. Subconsciousness. 2. Intuition (Psychology) 3. Intellect. 4. Conduct of life. 5. Psychotherapy—Case studies. I. Title.
BF315.H63 1994
154.2—dc20   94-28533
                                                      CIP

Printed in the United States of America

2 3 4 5 6 7 – 00 99 98 97 96 95

DEDICATION

To my daughters,

Tracy and Meredith,

two of my best teachers

with love

CONTENTS

ACKNOWLEDGMENTS

A book is always a team effort, in more ways than one can imagine, no matter how many hours there are alone for the author. I am grateful for my team.

First, there were the nurturers. My wife, Dorothy—with her encouragement, insight, and unselfishness for all the time I had to spend in my "mind cave" (as she calls my study)—was more than a partner. This is her book, too.

My brother, Greg, the real writer in the family, always unfailingly communicated his belief in my ideas. My publicist on my first book, Joyce Farrell, believed in me enough that I thought I could write another one. My good friends Arthur Evans, Ray Tyler, and Curt Moyes not only validated my work but also affirmed me. My friend Chuck Fromm gave me invaluable help along the way. And I would be remiss not to mention the late psychoanalyst Maurice Levine, M.D., who told me the first hour I met him that I was a writer. That left an indelible mark on me as a young intern.

Then there were my teachers. First and foremost would be Dr. Robert Langs, whose discovery of the great mind we all possess is at the heart of this book. I am also grateful to Bobby Frese, an editor on another, who helped me begin to learn to simplify technical ideas.

And there is my administrative staff, Sandy Weeks and Carolyn Marchant, who made sure everything was in place and on time.

And of course I am grateful to Thomas Nelson Publishers, those who had a vision for this book and without whom you would not be reading these pages. I am also very indebted to those who put the finishing touches on this book.

Last, I must thank my coach, my editor, Duncan Jaenicke, who helped me put this book in plain English, and in the process became a good friend by being one.

INTRODUCTION

One of the most important lessons I have learned in working with people in psychotherapy for over twenty years is to pay attention to details. That is perhaps the main reason I have been able to participate in one of the most exciting moments in the history of psychiatry, a time of a great breakthrough in our understanding of the mind.

In order to describe the breakthrough, I will frequently use clinical examples from psychotherapy because this is the environment where we study the mind and where our understanding of the deeper mind was first enlightened. The key points I make in most of these examples may at first seem to revolve around somewhat minor issues. Yet, it was an appreciation that these minor events were not really so minor that enabled the breakthrough to take place. (If we study history and look at breakthroughs in science, we will find that they often evolved from crucial but seemingly insignificant issues that had been overlooked.)

The primary application of the breakthrough to the mind is that we must look more closely at ourselves, not less closely. We must become more perceptive, not less. Actually, we must become more aware of the perceptions we have made "in the back of our minds" and learn how to better utilize them.

With the breakthrough to our deeper mind we have taken a quantum leap in self-understanding. We have discovered that our deeper mind itself knows a great deal it wants to share with our conscious mind.

At the heart of my work as a psychiatrist and psychotherapist is confidentiality. As a result I have gone to great lengths to preserve the privacy of any patient who has worked with me. All case studies in this book are presented with appropriate name changes and other disguises.

One thing will become clear to the readers. As human beings we all struggle with the same basic issues in life. In the end, this awareness should serve to heighten the respect we have for our neighbors as we will understand we are all soldiers in the same battle. Thus, the tendency to label people who see a therapist as sick or weak must diminish. Instead, they must be seen as individuals who have had the courage to try and face themselves and lead others to confront the same challenge.

Nature

loves to hide things.

Heraclitus, 500 B.C.

The answers are in nature.

It's up to us to find them.

Jonas Salk, medical researcher,
circa 1990

PART ONE

Understanding the Deeper Intelligence

CHAPTER ONE

What Is the Deeper Intelligence?

Although I didn't recognize it at the time, my first breathtaking encounter with the mysteries of the deeper intelligence occurred over two decades ago when I was a medical intern, learning the complexities of medicine.

It happened in the middle of the night. I was on call at a hospital, trying to catch a few hours of sleep after what seemed an endless string of exhausting days. A piercing noise jolted me from a sleep so deep that it took several moments before I remembered where I was. At the time I was covering the hospital's pediatrics unit. It had been a busy but relatively uneventful night up until then—no cardiac arrests, no respiratory crises, no sudden temperature spikes.

Yet what awaited me transcended the definition of "medical emergency." It would be one of the most striking experiences of my life.

The nurse on the other end of the line told me matter-of-factly, "Dr. Hodges, the twelve-year-old leukemic, Bobby Mason, in room 231, has just expired. He was a 'no code,' and we need you to come pronounce him dead and sign the death certificate."

Slowly the story came back to me. I had never seen

1

Bobby, but another intern, before going off duty, had briefly told me about him. Bobby had struggled for a long time with leukemia, and on this particular admission he clearly was terminal. The family had specifically requested that no resuscitation measures be taken when the end came (the "no code" medical designation). So Bobby died quietly in his room alone, perhaps a little sooner than the family had anticipated.

A few minutes after the nurse's call, I went to Bobby's room and carried out the perfunctory exam on his thin, pale body. Immediately afterward, I went to meet with his family. They had gathered in a small room near the nurses' station. I expected to find tears but also some relief. Yet, as often happens in life, the expected quickly becomes the unexpected.

The room was packed with relatives, none of whom I had ever met. Thinking that intuitively they all would know why the doctor wanted to see them in the middle of the night, I introduced myself and went straight to the point as compassionately as I could. The mother stood directly in front of me in the tiny room, her husband's arm around her. I purposefully focused my attention on her.

"I know you have been through a lot," I said. "No one can ever be completely prepared for something like this. I am sorry to have to tell you that Bobby passed away about twenty minutes ago. His suffering is over."

The mother, occasionally dabbing her eyes with a handkerchief, continued to stare at me in a puzzled, preoccupied manner as though she were trying to solve a problem. Finally, with some alarm in her voice, she insisted, "But doctor, aren't you going to give Bobby something for his cough?"

I thought perhaps she hadn't heard the words, "passed away." I looked at her again and said, "Mrs. Mason, I'm sorry, but Bobby just died a few minutes ago."

Her puzzled expression didn't change. She continued to

2

look at me, this time saying even more insistently, "But aren't you going to give him something for his cough?"

I was speechless. It was as though we were in separate worlds, speaking in languages the other couldn't understand. I had the strange feeling I could stand there forever because I couldn't get through to her—and as her son's doctor I was bound to stay until she understood the important but difficult news.

In that traumatic moment, as a young intern dealing with one of the most unique deaths I had encountered, I sensed how complicated are the ways of the human mind, that there is always much more going on than our conscious awareness seems to grasp or reveal.

Fortunately, the mother's family came to my rescue, and one of them said, "Doctor, you can go on with your duties. We will take care of her."

This striking experience was my first direct encounter with the two chambers of the human mind—a conscious chamber to handle what we can tolerate, and an unconscious chamber where we must bury traumas and unacceptable parts of ourselves. But several more years would pass before I truly understood the two distinct parts of the mind I had observed so poignantly as a mother struggled to accept the reality of her son's premature death.

THE BREAKTHROUGH TO THE DEEPER INTELLIGENCE

As a result of what many of us in the medical and psychiatric fields have discovered in patients, a revolutionary breakthrough in the understanding of how human beings function as has occurred. It is a life-changing concept that, in this book, I will call "the deeper intelligence." There is a capable part of our mind of which we are not immediately aware through our conscious feelings. It is a second compartment to the mind, and it functions in a way all its own. This part of our mind is commonly known as the subconscious or unconscious—but in truth it is a *deeper and more perceptive consciousness.* This hidden part of our mind is amazingly observant—truly a deeper intelligence—and it is always attempting to guide us, particularly at crucial moments in our lives.

This hidden part of our mind is amazingly observant—truly a deeper intelligence—and it is always attempting to guide us, particularly at crucial moments in our lives.

Almost everyone is familiar with the idea that we use only about 10 percent of our brain. It's like the proverbial tip of the iceberg. Both research and experience teach us that there are vast, untapped resources available to us. This is where the story of the breakthrough to the deeper intelligence begins. The deeper intelligence is essentially the other 90 percent of our mind.

In this book I will not attempt to document the full history of the important discovery of the deeper intelligence. However, a brief review of key events is necessary to provide a context for the exciting information that will follow.

PSYCHIATRY TODAY AND YESTERDAY

Modern psychiatry is actually less than 100 years old, going back to the time when Sigmund Freud began looking

4

deeper into the human mind. Freud (through his break-through work with dreams) was the first psychoanalyst to clarify that the mind had two distinct compartments—the conscious and the subconscious—which functioned separately.

Following Freud, psychology, broadly speaking, took two major branches—those who attempted to deal primarily with the subconscious mind or those who dealt mainly with the conscious mind. Among those therapists who focused primarily on the conscious mind were two major groups, behaviorists and counselors. Behaviorists attempted to control symptoms by instructing patients where to change their behavior and dealt almost exclusively with the conscious mind. Their motto was "don't worry about reasons, just fix it." Counselors used primarily conscious, cognitive techniques attempting to help patients "reason out" problems with their conscious mind amidst a warm, accepting environment.

On the other hand, analytic therapists attempted to deal with the subconscious mind and underlying motivations. Many therapists used a blend of these two methods, describing their approach as eclectic. Although eclectic therapists espoused the importance of flexibility, in actuality they lacked a consistent approach to psychological problems and were uncertain as to exactly what they were trying to accomplish and, thus, what really helped people.

In addition to these varied forms of individual therapy, different forms of group therapy emerged including conventional group therapy, marital therapy, and family therapy. In the last two decades, particularly, biological psychiatry has made its appearance as a third alternative. Here psychological problems are attributed to a chemical imbalance, and medication is seen as the wave of the future.

Into this hodgepodge of an environment came pioneer psychiatrist Robert Langs.[1] Although a psychoanalyst by training, Langs began his career in a medical center as a supervisor of therapists from many different schools of thought. He anticipated finding common threads of agreement and expected to find many different ways of solving psychological problems. Dr. Langs was remarkably open to therapists whose training was different from his own.

Indeed Langs did find his common thread among the different types of therapy, but it was different from what he had expected. He discovered an entirely new phenomenon—the deeper intelligence—and immediately recognized that therapists from all persuasions including his own (psychoanalysis) were overlooking it. The same deeper intelligence appeared no matter what the particular persuasion of the therapist. Furthermore, the deeper intelligence of each patient insisted on being approached in one consistent way to obtain maximum healing. Instead of finding many roads to the deeper mind and deep psychological healing, surprisingly, Langs had found one secret way.

Langs discovered that in the back of our minds, in our subconscious, we have a "secret observer"—a part of our mind that constantly and brilliantly evaluates our lives in a new way. It is a hundred times more perceptive and capable than our conscious mind in accurately analyzing the hundreds of messages we receive daily. Perhaps the most familiar example of the mind working in this fashion would be with subliminal advertising, where the deeper mind is allegedly picking up on many more messages than the conscious mind. As we will see, though, the deeper mind I am describing has far more ability than simply being capable of responding to hidden advertisements.

This observer, which I have labeled the deeper intelligence, continually picks up on a number of communications and subtle events in our lives which have powerful meanings for us and which our conscious mind overlooks. The deeper intelligence observes far more of reality than our conscious mind and communicates its observations in an exquisitely sensitive fashion in a special language of its own.

The deeper intelligence observes far more of reality than our conscious mind and communicates its observations in an exquisitely sensitive fashion in a special language of its own.

The deeper intelligence is the most brilliant, the most perceptive part of our mind. It is like a highly sophisticated radar capable of deciphering verbal and nonverbal communication, capable of seeing exactly what reality is in a given situation. Dr. Langs learned all about the deeper intelligence when he discovered its secret language. Once Langs broke the code to the deeper mind, he then understood its brilliance. (Previously, Freud had some awareness that the mind encoded messages, though Freud never completely broke the code to the deeper mind and thus never understood that we have a deeper intelligence.) Next Langs realized that this secret intelligence attempted to guide us in important decisions since its understanding is superior to our conscious mind. Our deeper intelligence knows, so to speak, where the treacherous parts of the road are and continually attempts to point us to the safest route.

This astounding discovery drastically changes how we view our deeper mind and thus ourselves. Rather than seeing our deeper mind as simply an emotional closet filled with unacceptable impulses and painful traumas, we now realize that we have the potential for accessing a brilliant, wise part of ourselves normally hidden from our awareness. This breakthrough offers enormous potential for personal growth and insight into ourselves.

Shortly after his breakthrough to the deeper intelligence, Langs made another startling discovery. Although the deeper intelligence continued to astound him with its phenomenal perceptive abilities, quite often patients consciously rejected the clear wisdom of their own deeper intelligence with disastrous consequences.

At this point Langs began to realize that there was a deep bent within people to suffer unnecessarily and an underlying tendency to make bad choices. Langs came to a significant understanding as to why this is so. He realized that there was another quite perceptive part of our deeper mind, which largely controlled our conscious mind (and decision making) and which tended to significantly overreact to (and reject) the healthy circumstances it needed. Although it is hard to believe that a part of our mind actually plans for us to suffer, once you see how its thinking gets distorted, you will understand why this is the case. Why this major distortion in our deeper mind occurs (I label it the "punishing intelligence") will be discussed later.

Langs discovered that our deeper intelligence always tries to show us a better way than the punishing intelligence, and if we listen to its wisdom, we can indeed overcome the negative influence of the punishing intelligence.

To demonstrate the kind of capability our deeper intelligence possesses, I want to relate an unusual occurrence in another branch of medicine where a physician made great use of our powerful hidden intelligence.

An Unusual Surgery

Seven figures stood quietly together, clad in wrinkled, dark green uniforms, gathered tightly around a ring of blazing white light. They had stood here—sternly and

8

intently working together—for nearly two hours straight. The surgeon and his assistant stood in silence over the husky patient lying helpless on the operating table. Peering out from behind their masks, the two surgeons were acutely aware of the many signals from the patient's body that could possibly be measured and observed. In every conceivable way, they were completely attuned to the young man whose life they held quite literally in their hands.

The chief surgeon made a routine glance at the heart monitor. Arising suddenly as a sharp interruption in this quiet drama, the patient's pulse had rapidly risen to one hundred and thirty. The doctor was well aware this could lead to cardiac irregularities or other complications. The worst scenario: It could threaten the patient's life.

What Dr. Bernie Siegel did next put a different spin on what to that point had been a routine operation. Normally he had two alternatives: Add another medication, which could present problems of its own because of side effects; or wait. Instead of choosing between the two, Dr. Siegel took a risk.

He remembered that the patient, Victor, had been more anxious than most people before surgery. With no other signs of trouble, was Victor's rising pulse rate his body's way of saying he was still nervous? Many surgeons don't appreciate how a patient's fears might carry over into the actual surgery. But Siegel did. Now he acted on his growing conviction.

Instead of uttering yet another command to his helpers, he addressed the patient, speaking calmly to Victor, who seemed to be many miles away in surgical anesthesia. Reassuringly, in fatherly tones, Dr. Siegel told Victor that the surgery was going fine and that everything would be all right. Then he told Victor the doctors needed his help. He told the patient his pulse had gotten too high at one hundred and thirty, and he asked Victor to bring it down to about eighty.

Several of the nurses did double takes, careful to not ignore their crucial duties for even a split second. A raised eyebrow here, a microscopic tilt of the head there. They must have wondered if the long hours and constant stress of high-stakes surgery had finally gotten to their award-winning chief surgeon.

Five minutes later, still engrossed in the surgery, Dr. Siegel asked, without looking up, "What's the pulse rate?"

The anesthesiologist replied, "Eighty-three."

"Eighty-three," repeated Dr. Siegel. Slowly, he began humming a tune to himself—and he wondered if Victor could hear the song too. The "helpless" patient, after all, wasn't really so helpless.

* * *

Dr. Bernie Siegel describes this scene (although I have taken some literary license) in his best-selling book, *Love, Medicine, and Miracles*.[2] Dr. Siegel also describes other cases in which doctors had effectively used the technique of speaking reassuringly to the "deeper mind" of patients who were under anesthesia. In one instance, one of Dr. Siegel's patients was seemingly beyond hope because he had failed to respond to resuscitation after suffering a post-surgery cardiac arrest. But Dr. Siegel spoke authoritatively to the patient—telling him to come back to life, that it was not his time to die yet. The man immediately began responding. Eventually he made a complete recovery.[3]

Although speaking to the part of the mind beyond immediate consciousness might seem otherworldly or somewhat "magical," the reason it works for Dr. Siegel and other surgeons like him has little to do with magic. I believe the same "deeper mind" which Dr. Siegel addressed so effectively in surgery is with us at all times—the deeper intelligence.

Just as Dr. Siegel discovered how to use the very capable part of our mind we are not conscious of in surgery, we have now discovered how to access the same deeper intelligence in psychotherapy. In therapy we not only can see this deeper mind at work, but we can hear it speak in its own unique language. The mind Dr. Siegel was successful in reaching was remarkably attuned to the patient's best interest and was able to guide the body in a very positive direction. Likewise in therapy, we now have available the same mind that functions independently of our conscious mind and guides us toward the healthiest mental functioning possible.

What I am telling you may sound strange, but after you are exposed to various instances of the deeper intelligence in action, you will find it truly remarkable—as I still do after working with the deeper intelligence for nearly twenty years on a daily basis.

WHAT THE DEEPER INTELLIGENCE IS AND ISN'T

Today, in an age of heightened media curiosity, we see a plethora of bizarre offerings about our nature as humans and our potential, dished up by a variety of thinkers having a wide range of credibility. I want to be absolutely clear that the deeper intelligence is *not* certain ideas such as reincarnation, channeling, and other so-called New Age phenomena involving another personality or some mystical spirit-guide. This kind of teaching often ends up, like Shirley MacLaine's philosophy, in the confusing and patently incorrect notion that human beings are God. In reality, the deeper intelligence is nothing mystical or magical. It is simply a part of our minds—a deeper part of our created being—that for the most part we aren't aware of.

I want to be absolutely clear that the deeper intelligence is not certain ideas such as reincarnation, channeling, and other so-called New Age phenomena involving another personality or some mystical spirit-guide.

The Bible states that humankind is made in the image of God—*Imago Dei*.[4] Yet misunderstanding over this incredible statement from the Scriptures is one reason why there is much confusion over the issue of individuals "being God." The Bible does not imply that we are in any way equal with God; rather, we simply bear His imprint. This imprint is so marvelous and mysterious that such confusion is easy to understand. Put another way, the deeper intelligence carries the Creator's thumbprint, but it is not His thumb.

Those people who believe humanity is made in the image of God have a perspective on humanity and creation that is inherently big enough to accept that there is a deeper intelligence. Think about it: Our mind is the most impressive thing about our identity; it reflects our Maker like no other part. And our deeper intelligence is simply a phenomenally gifted part of our minds which reflects that we are truly made in the image of God.

While an awareness of the deeper intelligence reveals the greatness of humankind in a way we have never seen before, it also keeps us humble, because it shows our frailties and imperfections in an entirely new way. For example, it shows not only our incredible power of perception, but deception, too—our incredible capability for deceiving both others and ourselves.

As we all know, it is very difficult to own up to personal failure and admit we are wrong. As C. S. Lewis said, "It takes a good man to repent—and we are all bad men."[5] Those who are most easily able to acknowledge their imperfections will be better able to accept and benefit from the discovery of their deeper intelligence.

We must understand that the remarkable part of ourselves that is the deeper intelligence is *the ultimate realist*. It encourages us to recognize our greatness as never before, and yet it also asks of us that we face *all* of ourselves; it asks us to neither think too lowly of ourselves nor too highly. Indeed, the deeper intelligence is a master at helping us define our true identity, helping us see who we really are—and who we really aren't. It also insists that we take responsibility for our actions no matter how much we've been influenced by others.

As we will see, this question of our identity affects virtually all of our relationships. Much too often, for instance, we lose perspective on where our responsibility begins and ends with others, causing us to involve ourselves in codependent relationships. The deeper intelligence helps us to see there is far more to our interactions with each other than we have appreciated. This is true as well with our primary relationship—our spiritual one—with our Creator (whether we consciously think we have a relationship with our Creator or not).

In the final analysis, our deeper intelligence is the most logical, down-to-earth part of ourselves—the ultimate realist—because *it sees clearly what is going on*. Why this part of our minds is hidden from us is one of the mysteries we will explore.

NEED FOR A NEW PARADIGM

What we need in thinking about the deeper intelligence is a paradigm shift. We must learn how to listen to ourselves and others all over again—to listen in a completely new way. We need "new ears" to hear the spoken messages from the deeper intelligence, since it communicates in a different language. The same challenge that Jesus once brought to his listeners—"He who has ears, let him hear"—exists for us today.[6] Unfortunately, as history has recorded time and again, many of us do not "have ears to hear." We simply do not want to accept new insights—even if the information potentially is of great benefit to us. For example, in 1983, geneticist Dr. Barbara McClintock won the Nobel Prize in Physiology and Medicine. Some consider her the foremost biologist of this century and the most important geneticist since Gregor Mendel, the father of modern genetics. Yet Dr. McClintock's revolutionary discoveries in genetics, going back to the 1940s, were ignored for years because her findings were difficult to fit into old paradigms. Only now are they being incorporated as the study of genetics continues to develop. To begin to reap the benefits the deeper intelligence offers, we must appreciate our difficulty accepting change and new information.

The significance of the discovery of the language of the deeper intelligence, as well as the fact that it has gone somewhat overlooked, is like an anecdote I recently read in a George Will column. Entitled, "Important Events Take Time to Recognize," it dealt with the beginnings of the development of the atomic bomb during World War I. In 1918, when Dr. Ernest Rutherford, a New Zealand physicist working in England, missed a meeting being held to study defenses against German submarines, he was upbraided for his oversight. He replied, "Talk softly, please. I have been engaged in experiments which suggest that the atom can be artificially disintegrated. If that is true, it is of far greater importance than a war." I'm sure his colleagues, especially the nonscientists, raised an eyebrow or two and thought him overly dramatic. Yet history

14

proved him right, and it was only a matter of time before the impact of his discovery was borne out.[7]

I am quite sure that history will treat similarly the significance of the deeper intelligence. The profundity of the guidance that it provides, combined with the other extraordinary functions which we will examine in the next few chapters, is life changing at the very least. Still it will take time.

The noted physicist Max Planck once commented that the greater a discovery, the more the opposition to it as a new idea. He felt that there is a direct correlation with the resistance a pioneer runs up against: The more change the new discovery demands, the more resistance is found.

Just as Dr. McClintock was finally recognized for her contributions to genetics, I believe that one day Dr. Langs will receive his just recognition as a true genius in the field of psychology—perhaps the greatest contributor to date. It is not extreme to predict that eventually his influence will surpass that of Freud, Carl Jung, and others.

Yet all of us are tempted to resist innovation. As a result of our discomfort with new knowledge about ourselves and because we live in a sophisticated society, we, too, have a tendency to think that there is no room left for truly major discoveries. Probably every generation has felt the same way. But if we are to profit from the major discovery of the deeper intelligence, we must at least be open to the idea that a major paradigm shift in our understanding of the mind has occurred.

However, one important thing must be remembered about the deeper intelligence: *It is not something "new" in us; it is only a new way of seeing what we've had all along.* This book is meant to help us comprehend a long-misunderstood part of our minds, not a new part of our minds. Like our physical body, our mind has a built-in process whereby it attempts to heal itself. The deeper intelligence attempts to draw our attention to problem

15

areas that beset us, and it encourages us to take the paths in life that are truly in our best interest.

In light of this discovery, we must ask ourselves some difficult but potentially eye-opening questions. I challenge you to consider these as you read this book:

- Is it possible that each of us has a brilliant part of our mind that is hidden from us? Are we willing to consider that there is more to our personality than we now know?
- Can we admit that at any given moment our feelings—no matter how strong they are—can deceive and mislead us?
- Do we really *want* to know the rest of ourselves? Do we really *want* to see who we are? Do we have the courage and bravery to venture into these uncharted waters?
- Do we *want* to profit from our deeper intelligence?

This brings up my purposes in writing this book:

1. I want to show clearly that a deeper intelligence exists in each of us and is active in our lives moment by moment.
2. I want to show how much more is involved in our daily communication and to help you begin to develop an ear for the deeper intelligence.
3. I want to show how the deeper intelligence reveals clear principles for living on a daily basis—principles upon which deep down we all agree. Often, unknowingly, we have blind spots that greatly contribute to our own (and others') suffering, which can be overcome with the help of the deeper intelligence.
4. I will discuss how the deeper intelligence points us toward a healthy spirituality. I will show how true psychology and true faith, far from being enemies, are in the final analysis highly compatible.

I will show how true psychology and true faith, far from being enemies, are in the final analysis highly compatible.

Only seekers find. And if you do decide to seek, your deeper intelligence promises that eventually you will have startling and satisfying insights into your true self. These insights probably won't come suddenly. But if you can begin to acknowledge right now that you know only about 10 percent of your deepest motivations, then you will be on your way to new and helpful insights.

Just think about it! If what I am telling you is true, it means that we all possess at all times a powerful mind with which we are not in immediate contact, a mind which manifests itself in disguised ways, which attempts to guide us in ways that benefit us significantly, and which knows clearly the best path to take. If we could learn how to access that mind and heed its guidance, it could be of untold benefit to ourselves and mankind in general. That is the core purpose of this book and an exciting prospect indeed.

CHAPTER TWO

The Two Chambers of the Mind

In 1899, in his revolutionary book on dreams,[1] Austrian psychiatrist Sigmund Freud firmly established that the human mind has two separate chambers—a conscious and a subconscious—which function independently of each other and utilize two different languages to communicate.

As I begin to tell you of the breakthrough to the deeper intelligence, at first you may wonder if what I am describing is really a breakthrough since the deeper intelligence, buried in our subconscious mind, utilizes symbolic communication and indirect messages just as Freud previously observed.

While there are some similarities between the discovery of the deeper intelligence and Freud's work, the difference is like night and day. In my opinion Freud and his successors never understood the language of the deeper mind. Indeed Freud, the alleged master of the subconscious, repeatedly failed to comprehend the deeper intelligence's clear messages. He saw the deeper mind only as an emotional closet of sorts, where we keep our fears and forbidden wishes. He missed the gold mine on which he was sitting.

18

*He (Freud) saw the deeper mind
only as an emotional closet of sorts,
where we keep our fears and forbidden
wishes. He missed the gold mine on
which he was sitting.*

Yet Freud was the first person to stake out the second
level of our mind as clearly a separate entity. He was the
first to hear the voice of the deeper mind; he just didn't
understand what it was saying. It wasn't until 1973 that
Robert Langs began to understand and clarify the messages sent by the deeper mind. As you might expect with
a psychiatrist, Dr. Langs's insights first surfaced in a
therapy session.[2]

On a gray winter day some years ago in New York City,
Dr. Langs was listening intently to a patient, Sally. While
seemingly drifting rather casually from one subject to
another, Sally was actually speaking eloquently with
great conviction, revealing the core of her character. Dr.
Langs was noting carefully her every word, trying to put
together a pattern from her thoughts that might help.

As the session had begun that day, Sally had asked the
doctor to speak briefly with her husband to reassure him.
She had noted to her therapist, "My husband is very
protective, and he sometimes has a problem trusting.
Although he won't admit it, he feels anxious about my
being alone with you, another man, discussing personal
things."

As usual Dr. Langs had allowed his patient to continue
talking. He wanted to see if there was more to her request
than met the ear initially. Certainly he was aware that
Sally saw her husband as overprotective and jealous at
times. Yet while her request might genuinely reflect her

husband's anxiety about her being alone with a therapist. Dr. Langs wondered if Sally herself didn't have a deeper issue in addition to her husband's.

In his experience as a psychotherapist, Dr. Langs had become increasingly interested in the seemingly small events that took place within the therapy room. His intuition told him there usually was a more profound meaning to certain events that directly involved the therapist—for example a simple request to borrow a pen, use the phone, or change an appointment time. He was dissatisfied with the way other therapists seemed to overanalyze or oversimplify these things. Dr. Langs had the distinct hunch that if he treated these things too casually, he would miss something very significant.

Suddenly Sally caught his attention as she began talking about a seemingly unrelated situation. Casually, she mentioned, "The other day I had planned to have a private talk about a personal issue with a good friend over lunch. But then, unannounced, my girlfriend brought along a coworker, spoiling our privacy. I can't believe she could be so insensitive."

Dr. Langs recognized a possible connection between Sally's mention of her lunchtime incident and her therapy. She had talked about her girlfriend spoiling an important one-to-one relationship by bringing in a third party, just after she had asked her therapist to speak with her husband—which also involved bringing in a third party who possibly could interfere with a key one-to-one relationship, that of the patient and doctor. Dr. Langs wondered to himself if the connection was valid. He decided to keep listening for confirmation.

The evidence was not long in coming. A few minutes later, Sally said, "The other day my five-year-old daughter was enjoying herself playing with a friend when suddenly a third child joined them, and she became crabby. Two's company, but three's a crowd, I guess."

Here's another thought about a third party interfering

20

in a relationship, the doctor thought. *Is it possible this woman's mind really knows what is best and is trying to guide us to keep her husband out of her therapy? I'm not going to believe it unless she tells me one more story about unwanted threesomes.*

Only a few minutes later Sally, seemingly just rambling, commented, "I love my mother-in-law, but my husband took some of the joy out of our last vacation by having her go along. It prevented us from having some needed time alone together."

By this time, Dr. Langs was astounded. He concluded to himself, *Deep down, this patient really knows what is best for her. Sally is taking what seems to be a minor event—my meeting with her husband—and showing me that it is not so minor. Her mind is insisting upon using the canvas it has to work with—telling stories in therapy— to paint a living picture of what is bothering her, so she can be healed.*

Dr. Langs had deciphered this "coded message" that meant Sally didn't believe third parties were helpful in key one-to-one relationships. He was well on the way to discovering the voice of the deeper intelligence. But one aspect puzzled him: *Why would she present a request to me—to meet with her husband—that conflicted with her real needs?*

The answer, Dr. Langs later concluded, had to do with anxiety about intimate relationships—a core element in understanding our deeper minds. Sally told another story that explained her motivation. She spoke of a friend who was breaking off her marital engagement, which Sally attributed to the girlfriend's fearing close relationships. As Sally described it, "I don't think anything was really wrong with the guy she was marrying. I just think she can't handle closeness."

Now Dr. Langs had all the pieces of the puzzle, and he could make his interpretation to Sally. He pointed out to her that since she'd made the request for him to meet with her husband, her thoughts had repeatedly headed to ideas of third parties unknowingly interfering in relationships. He also told her that she was not only saying it *wouldn't* be a good idea to meet with her husband, but that she was nervous about being alone in a one-to-one relationship with him (her doctor), as evidenced in her telling him about the friend who feared marriage.

Sally initially protested the validity of this interpretation. But shortly afterward, she talked for the first time about a frightening childhood experience she'd had at a summer camp when she had been alone in the woods and run into a strange man. *Here's another example of her anxiety about close relationships,* Dr. Langs thought. Langs did not appreciate at that time that he had discovered the primary fear which controls human behavior—security anxiety—which I will elaborate on later.

As if he didn't have enough indirect evidence to confirm his hunches, Sally closed the session by talking about how her husband was really a good man and a particularly good listener despite his other faults. At this point, Dr. Langs realized he had struck gold. By her last comment, Sally was thanking him indirectly for catching on. She had said, in effect, "When you learn how to listen to my deeper mind, you are helping me. Thanks."

As Dr. Langs shared how her last comments fit in, Sally began to comprehend a little better just what was going on. It was still to her a totally new way of interpreting her stories. But it was new to Dr. Langs, too.

From that session onward, Dr. Langs began to realize he was truly on to something. As the years went by, he developed the theory and practice of recognizing the deeper intelligence, and he began to share it with his colleagues (including me). He decided he would now listen to his patients with new respect. If indeed Sally's deeper mind had been trying to guide him, surely other patients' minds had, too. It would have been easy to miss what Sally was really telling him and to go along with her request to

22

invade their crucial privacy by inviting in the nervous husband.

The great breakthrough to the deeper intelligence had begun.

He had discovered the special story-telling language which the deeper intelligence uses to bring about its own healing.

Little did Dr. Langs know at the time that he would confirm his findings with patient after patient—a deeper, wiser part of every patient was constantly trying to guide every therapy to bring about healing. Only later would he fully realize that he had discovered the deeper intelligence, that he was the first man to break the code—the specific language—to the deeper mind.

He had discovered its *actual voice*. He had discovered the special storytelling language which the deeper intelligence uses to bring about its own healing. Eventually, when he learned to consistently hear it speak, Dr. Langs would be so impressed with the deeper intelligence he would state, "Working with the subconscious mind is like listening to an omniscient being."[3]

From the very first moment the deeper intelligence became real for me, I was convinced that it perfectly describes the magnificent mind Robert Langs discovered, even though he didn't coin the term. (While the story of Sally represents a composite case study—Dr. Langs doesn't reveal specific incidents about his patients for confidentiality purposes—for all practical purposes, it is what happened. I know this because I have heard him describe the breakthrough in general terms. I have observed Dr. Langs demonstrate the breakthrough to the deeper intelligence in hundreds of cases with other therapists' patients in teaching situations. And I have watched as numerous therapists, including myself, have validated his findings.)

The Key to Langs's Discovery: Trigger Decoding

Robert Langs discovered what all previous doctors of the mind had overlooked—the meaning of seemingly simple "reality events" within the therapy itself, events that took place in front of the therapist. By recognizing reality on the second level of the mind, the deeper mind, he could compare it to the first level, the patient's conscious or perceived reality. Thus, Sally's conscious mind saw the reality event of bringing her husband into her sessions as harmless. But her deeper mind saw it, as revealed through her stories, as a third-party intrusion that threatened to spoil an important one-to-one relationship. This new understanding of the hidden meaning of a reality event enabled Dr. Langs to gain insight into who people really are deep down.

In essence, Dr. Langs grasped how the mind took a seemingly small reality in the smaller part of the mind (the conscious mind) to define a larger reality in the largest part of the mind (the subconscious mind).

Time after time, as different "minor" reality events

24

came up in therapy, Langs could see their deeper meaning because he now knew how to listen. He constantly compared the reality event to the stories the patient told—and he grew to better understand the great link. Once he comprehended that the reality events triggered the stories the patient told, he understood them to be a key to the workings of the deeper mind at a particular moment.

In essence, Dr. Langs grasped how the mind took a seemingly small reality in the smaller part of the mind (the conscious mind) to define a larger reality in the largest part of the mind (the subconscious mind). By continually observing these small events in therapy, he learned to his amazement, time after time, that they had important meanings for the patient.

Before he had made his discovery, Langs was like many other therapists who read messages into the deeper mind that weren't there, and at the same time overlooked messages that were there—all because he didn't have the key to understanding them. (For example, he might interpret a patient coming late to an appointment as being uncooperative when, in fact, the patient was secretly terrified of him.)

Langs eventually would refer to these little events as "triggers." And as he continued to keep his eye on these triggers, he discovered that he now had three tools with which to work: (1) the key to the second part of the mind—a reality event he could observe, a trigger; (2) the code the deeper mind used—i.e., seemingly unrelated stories—to communicate exactly how the trigger event affected it; and (3) access to the phenomenal deeper intelligence. Through these three elements, he discovered that reality on the deeper level of our mind is far more critical than either the patient or the doctor realizes. In short, Dr. Langs discovered that patients have a need to give a live demonstration of their key issues in therapy—just as Sally had done—in order to obtain an immediate cure, something they can only get from a healthy therapist who understands their unconscious motives and needs.

Idea Language

Langs realized that the two parts of the mind utilized two distinct languages. The conscious mind communicated in a literal language—"I want you to speak to my husband." The deeper mind communicated in an indirect language, an idea language. For example, as we just witnessed, after Sally's conscious mind made a literal request, her deeper mind communicated a number of indirect messages which conveyed the thought, "Don't meet with my husband [because it would create an unhealthy threesome]."

The conscious mind communicated in a literal language—"I want you to speak to my husband." The deeper mind communicated in an indirect language, an idea language.

Sally used a number of seemingly unrelated literal stories about others to convey one consistent idea about herself. By paying attention not just to a literal comment but noting what ideas came to Sally's mind *and when*, Langs discovered just how precisely the deeper mind could speak.

When certain ideas came to mind was what Freud had overlooked. He consistently missed out on the full meaning of the ideas from the deeper mind, because he would repeatedly overlook a particular event which had triggered a certain train of thought. Usually he did so because the events themselves were errors he was making in therapy and couldn't face. Because he was not open to the ideas of the deeper mind, ideas which indicated the deeper intelligence "saw through him," Freud never understood how capable the deeper mind was.

Carl Jung, originally a disciple of Freud and later a rival, had a greater appreciation for the innate abilities of the deeper mind, and this has carried over to Jung's followers to this day. Jungian therapists talk about the subconscious mind possessing a great deal of innate wisdom, but when it comes to actually listening to the deeper intelligence, Jungians are in practice no different than Freudians. They have failed to appreciate precisely how capable and active the deeper intelligence is because they, too, have not understood the specific second language of the deeper mind. David Smith, a brilliant British psychotherapist makes this case in professional journals and in his recent book *Hidden Conversations* as he points out that Jungians and Freudians alike have overlooked the deeper intelligence.[4]

As far as understanding the second language of the mind, Jung and Freud both could be compared to an Englishman who wasn't conversant in French but recognized an occasional word or phrase. On the other hand, Langs would represent someone fluent in both languages.

The irony in all of this is that a number of well-known therapists or schools of therapy talk a great deal about the second level of the human mind, despite the fact that they have overlooked the deeper intelligence. Along these lines, many therapists and others repeatedly mention the importance of taking a holistic (from the Greek meaning "whole") approach to the mind, while simultaneously tuning out the voice of the deeper intelligence that really opens up the ninety percent of our mind that is hidden.

Precursors to the Breakthrough to Deeper Intelligence

Before the breakthrough to the magnificent territory of the deeper intelligence, there was a growing awareness that the human mind was a great frontier yet to be conquered. Many sensed that our minds possess far more potential than we seem able to harness. A striking recognition of the potential of the deeper mind came from biologist and science writer Lewis Thomas, who called for a breakthrough to our "super-intelligence" based on the observation that many times hypnotized patients have been able to cure their own warts.

As Thomas noted, "You can't sit there under hypnosis, taking suggestions in and having them acted on with such accuracy and precision, without assuming the existence of something very much like a controller. . . . Some intelligence or other knows how to get rid of warts, and this is a disquieting thought. It is also a wonderful problem in need of solving. Just think what we would know if we had anything like a clear understanding of what goes on when a wart is hypnotized away . . . *we would be finding out about a kind of super-intelligence that exists in each of us, infinitely smarter and possessed of technical know-how far beyond our present understanding.* It would be worth a War on Warts, a Conquest of Warts, a National Institute of Warts and all."[5]

THE SECRET STORYTELLER: RIGHT BRAIN AND LEFT BRAIN

The discovery of the deeper intelligence parallels other work presently going on concerning the mind, in particular the focus on the differences between our "right brain" and "left brain." The fact that our mind communicates on

28

two levels at the same time is closely related to the idea of our right and left brain functioning in different ways.

As a result of various studies in recent years, it has become popular to conceptualize the two sides of the brain as having different functions. The left side is thought of as the reasonable, analytical, logical, factual, and task-oriented side, whereas the right side appears to be intuitive, creative, emotional, relational, and artistic.

Communication styles also appear to be dictated by these different halves of our brain. It is commonly held that the left hemisphere uses a straightforward, literal, just-the-facts sort of style, while the right brain communicates more indirectly, symbolically, and creatively, often using word pictures or stories. Typically, women are considered to be more right-brain-focused, while men are seen as more left-brain-dominant—a myth the deeper intelligence largely dispels. Now that we can see right-brain communication clearly in therapy, it is obvious that both men *and* women are phenomenally gifted at right-brain communication. *For the sake of conceptualizing that our mind constantly communicates on these two basic levels, I will consistently make the somewhat arbitrary distinction that subconscious or deeper intelligence communication is right-brain communication. Likewise, I will consistently refer to conscious communication as left-brain communication.*

Typically, women are considered to be more right-brain-focused, while men are seen as more left-brain-dominant—a myth the deeper intelligence largely dispels.

Certain therapists have attempted to engage the right side of the brain more frequently. This has resulted in various therapeutic techniques, such as encouraging patients to communicate with others using images or stories instead of direct communication. Marriage counselors Gary Smalley and John Trent, in their best-selling book *The Language of Love*, encourage couples to use what they call emotional word pictures—made-up, brief, emotionally-charged stories to communicate feelings, in order to enrich communication and grasp what the other person is feeling.[6]

For example, a wife, instead of telling her husband directly that he is insensitive to her feelings, would say something like, "When you are critical of me, I feel like a beautiful, peaceful garden of spring flowers whose normally tender gardener has suddenly come in and pulled up all the flowers and trampled them."

Such techniques deal almost exclusively with the conscious chamber of the mind. Nevertheless, these efforts point us in an important direction, one that enables us to understand the breakthrough to the other level of our mind. Simply put, the deeper intelligence possesses a magnificent storyteller that it uses to critique our lives at crucial times.

When we are able to "hear" the deeper intelligence, we find that it speaks in a remarkably specific way.

When we are able to "hear" the deeper intelligence, we find that it speaks in a remarkably specific way. For example, a friend of mine named John was contemplating a job change with great trepidation. It involved not only a geographic move but also meant working with a very successful but extremely difficult business partner. We spent a considerable period of time discussing the pros and cons of the move one night, and the next day John told me that he had had a dream about an earthquake which wrecked his house and greatly endangered his family.

In the same conversation (yet not talking specifically about his dream), John talked about people he knew who foolishly moved to San Francisco after all the earthquakes that had occurred there. He knew about my work with the deeper intelligence, and I knew him well enough to suggest that through his dream and his comments about moving to the San Francisco Bay area, perhaps he was trying to tell himself something about what the move might hold for him and his loved ones. He laughed nervously and said he saw the connection. Shortly thereafter, he decided to take the lucrative job offer.

Despite significant material benefits, the move turned out in many ways to be devastating to his family. John's partner was even more nightmarish to work with than he had imagined. And as a result of the constant pressure he was under at work, John became irritable and at times uncharacteristically explosive at home. His marriage was severely threatened, and his children were greatly upset by the turmoil. *It was not unlike an earthquake had hit the family.* John's deeper intelligence had clearly tried to warn him—with a dream, with a story, with the urge to seek the advice of a friend, with his own intuition. Yet he had chosen to ignore all of these sources of possible wisdom, to his great detriment.

Our deeper intelligence has extraordinary abilities. Every second of our lives our deeper mind is scanning our environment, both internal and external, picking up all sorts of messages and events that our left brain misses. Our right brain is particularly attentive to relationships and is capable of deciphering multiple meanings from one or two reality events and clarifying which of the meanings is most important. Indeed, the right brain is a master at getting the whole picture and determining exactly what reality is.

To appreciate our deeper intelligence we must recognize that it virtually always communicates indirectly through ideas, through analogies.

To appreciate our deeper intelligence we must recognize that it virtually always communicates indirectly through ideas, through analogies. For example John's deeper intelligence knew enough about him and the environment that he was headed for to say through a dream that the move would be as devastating to his stability as an earthquake. Later his mind tried to warn him again and used an analogy of people who made foolish moves into dangerous areas. Ideas—analogies and comparisons—are the way the deeper intelligence speaks. In many ways this right-brain creativity is a far richer form of communication than left-brain literalness.

You may be wondering: Is the idea of intuition part of, or the same as, the deeper intelligence? No—the latter is far more than our intuition, although intuition can be our deeper mind expressing itself. The deeper intelligence might be thought of as *hidden* intuition.

As we come to see the principles by which the deeper intelligence operates, we will have a much clearer picture of when it is speaking and what messages are being communicated. The challenge before us is to learn how to hear those messages.

CHAPTER THREE

The Three Core Functions of the Deeper Intelligence

"It is the glory of God to conceal a matter,
But the glory of kings is to search out a matter."
Prov. 25:2, NKJV

I couldn't get through to David. There he sat before me, confident, bright, articulate, energetic, persistent—winsomeness radiating from him. He was an aggressive businessman in his early fifties who had recently started his own consulting business, a man unafraid of taking risks. There was only one problem: David was losing in his new business and he needed to learn how to win.

David and I had been good friends for a while. This meant I couldn't possibly see him as a patient. Being a friend prevents me from also being a therapist. But I agreed to work with him as an informal business consultant.

At one point in my career I had become interested in what enables certain people to achieve their goals and why others fall short. This led me to a fascinating study on leadership and success, broadly defined. Everybody is in the business of trying to succeed at something—that is, to accomplish a cherished goal—whether they are in business, involved in a professional career, raising children, pursuing academics, or devoting themselves to the ministry.

David recently had realized that despite his considerable talent, he had a problem obtaining success commensurate with his abilities in his new business. We began to meet somewhat regularly, to review certain basic management principles and discuss potential blind spots. It quickly became apparent that David was "defeating himself," though certainly not from a lack of effort. He was working hard, but he wasn't working smart.

In several key areas, David had developed blind spots. First, he tended to "micro-manage," which meant he was always putting out fires. This blind spot left him always focusing on the short run, the immediate, and kept him from developing his business to anything near the degree to which he could have. David also was failing to set clear-cut goals for his business. He tended to become over involved with each client without regard to a schedule or a budget.

Although he began to get an overall picture of where he needed to make changes, he continued to drag his feet in following through. He failed to establish a clear plan for expanding his business and was slow to carry out the plans he did make. Over and over, he insisted he just hated to be confined to a rigid schedule and "to do things like everyone else does."

Yet, grudgingly, through our talks he slowly began to see that the price he was paying for his ineffective management style was too great. It was at this point, when David was caught between his better judgment and his personality tendencies, that we had a key meeting.

David came bounding into the room in his usual optimistic, buoyant fashion—but almost immediately he began telling me about a very frustrating meeting he recently had had with a client. David said, "He just can't make up his mind about what he wants to do. His business has incredible potential, but as C.E.O. he's holding the whole company back. He could make some decisions now which would significantly benefit his company, but he's as stubborn as a mule and won't go ahead with them. It will probably be six months before he comes up with a plan. He could make the key decisions tomorrow, but I don't think he will."

For several minutes, David continued to ventilate about his client. Eventually he began addressing his own management issues. While he thought he was making some progress, I knew he still had a long way to go in carrying out his plan. Then suddenly there occurred to me a new way to help David—a way with real potential.

There was no question in my mind that David's deeper intelligence was trying to get his attention as he told the story of his frustrating, change-resistant client. This anecdote was a clear description of exactly what David was doing with his own company. Although I was trying to help David as a consultant and friend—not a therapist—it seemed David had implicitly given me permission to point out his blind spots. Since addressing blind spots is the essence of the deeper intelligence's work, and I knew David was aware of the workings of the deeper mind, I decided it was appropriate for me to make a comment to him. I realized David had told me the story of the change-resistant client for a purpose. *He was using me to help him see himself.*

You may wonder why *David* couldn't see the connection between his client and himself. This is the nature of blind spots, but someone who is not emotionally involved in your personal issues usually can see your blind spots better than you can. But how could I be so sure David's deeper intelligence was really talking about him? Don't people naturally talk about frustrations with their friends? Might that have been a coincidence? I can only say that after much experience with the deeper intelligence, I have observed that it operates *consistently to select the best available story to communicate its observations.*

Here's what I said: "David, you know that you're not really making the changes you need to make in your business. I want you to think about something. Perhaps we have just witnessed your deeper intelligence at work in trying to help you get ahead. That story you told about your frustrating client could also be your own mind trying to show you yourself. If that's the case, your unconscious mind is telling you that deep down you're planning on prolonging your misery for six months. You don't have to continue to frustrate yourself that long, though, if you hear your own words and do something about following through with your plans."

As I spoke, David's usually self-assured expression changed to one of bewilderment and discomfort. Had I not been a therapist, it would have been one of the strangest expressions I had ever seen: Both shock and yearning registered on his face. I often witness this unusual combination of emotions when people meet their deeper intelligence. When we truly come face-to-face with that deep, inner part of us, we are indeed shocked—and yet something in us wants to continue hearing from it, even though it may be painful. Listening to the deeper mind is like listening to someone else talk about you, someone who is amazingly perceptive and cuts through to your real motivations. It feels eerie and even scary at first, but once you realize it's really *you* talking about *you*, it seems right and you want to know more.

When we truly come face-to-face with that deep, inner part of us, we are indeed shocked—and yet something in us wants to continue hearing from it, even though it may be painful.

That is the power the deeper intelligence exerts upon

you—when you let it. It's like coming into contact with a wise person. Your life is never the same afterward, because you have been confronted gently, yet powerfully, with much truth.

David finally heard me—or, I should say, he heard *himself*. And from that day onward, there was a clear difference in the way he planned and ran his business. Despite his continuing battle with his personality tendencies, he made significant strides in setting goals. And, as a result, his business increased significantly.

Actually, David had received guidance from one of the three core functions of the deeper intelligence. I call them the *guidance mode*, the *boundary mode*, and the *stabilizing mode*.

THE DEEPER INTELLIGENCE OFFERS GUIDANCE

This first part of the deeper mind—the guidance mode—is like a phenomenal observer who analyzes every situation in which we find ourselves and constantly tries to lead us in the healthiest direction. The guidance mode is often observed in psychotherapy. For example, a patient states she has come to a decision to stop her sessions, feeling she has learned everything that she needs to know about herself. After assuring her therapist she has thought the decision through, she says she feels certain it is time to stop.

This is what I call "proposing Plan A."

However, a patient will in the same session give clues that her deeper intelligence has a better plan—a Plan B—if she senses deep down that she has other issues to resolve. If she cooperates and gives her deeper mind a chance to communicate (by simply going ahead and talking), she will eventually talk about people who don't finish jobs, who fail to graduate, who don't obtain everything they can out of a situation, who don't close sales, who do things halfway, who quit school just when they need more education. This is the deeper intelligence's *guidance mode* in action. This mode virtually always knows best. (In many cases, when a person's deeper intelligence knows it is time to stop therapy, the guidance mode will confirm this by prompting the patient to tell stories of completed tasks, jobs well done, graduations, and the like—a "job is finished" code.)

The benefits of knowing how to listen for the guidance mode are great. In short, there are two types of dilemmas we face daily: Those we are consciously aware of and those we are not aware of. The latter occur much more often than we think, since hidden dilemmas are just that—hidden. That is exactly what I illustrated above. The patient who wanted to stop therapy had no idea a dilemma even existed; in her mind, she had done the work she had come to do, and that was all there was to it.

The guidance mode attempts to *heighten your awareness of dilemmas*. For example, you might be certain you have correctly assessed a problem in your marriage as your spouse's fault. Yet the guidance mode may have observed that unknowingly you are making a hidden, negative contribution to the relationship. Thus, you consciously think the primary problem is issue A, but subconsciously your guidance mode knows it's primarily issue B.

It's a troubling thought, but often our conscious mind lies to us. I believe this is one of the meanings of the biblical proverb, "There is a way that seems right to a man / But its end is the way of death," (Prov. 16:25 NKJV). Phrased differently, this means that just because a certain option may *seem* right doesn't necessarily make it the best one.

This limitation in our conscious thinking can affect all of our relationships. We all possess blind spots in our marriage, in our parent-child relationships (particularly with our teenagers), in our business relationships, and in our friendships. The guidance mode serves to open up to us all sorts of possibilities, both exciting and threatening.

While discussing the subject of blind spots, I must mention a disturbing trend developing in psychiatry (and echoing into psychology in general). Far too many professionals are telling us we are just biological creatures. They feel that virtually the entire future of psychology is biology, in regulating brain chemistry through medication. The drug Prozac has come to symbolize this development, highlighted in Peter Kramer's recent book, *Listening to Prozac*, which points out many of the benefits of this drug.[1]

Listening to the deeper intelligence offers at least as much, if not more, potential benefit for easing emotional suffering (and to society in general) than "listening to Prozac."

As a doctor who has prescribed Prozac several hundred times, I am well familiar with its benefits and limitations. For many people, Prozac or any other medication is hardly the last word in treatment, as Kramer acknowledges in his book. I have seen many patients on Prozac whose deeper intelligence told me there was far more to their problem than what Prozac was addressing—even when they were doing better. As we will see, any medication that we must depend upon is less than ideal. Medication does not represent the entire wave of the future in psychology or psychiatry. Listening to the deeper intelligence offers at least as much, if not more, potential benefit for easing emotional suffering (and to society in general) than "listening to Prozac." (Interestingly, in a recent *Newsweek*

39

article about Prozac, several psychiatrists talked about patients who went off their Prozac but stayed in therapy as they had the sense that they could better understand themselves off medication.[2]) The deeper intelligence is the latest development in our understanding of the mind—the cutting edge. In the future it will continue to be at the heart of what we learn about the mind, because it is the heart of the mind.

We now know that the second chamber of our mind is no longer some vague amorphous part of us, but rather is a brilliant separate part of our mind that speaks clearly in its own language and offers profound guidance. Knowing this enables us to multiply our knowledge about ourselves. We have what Langs called a "psychoscope," which enables us to look deep into our minds. Just as the microscope reveals to us a hidden world teeming with life, the discovery of the "psychoscope" reveals to us the hidden world of our deeper mind, where far more is going on than we ever imagined.

We can now study various events—such as a proposal to stop therapy, or a married couple suggesting a trial separation, or a thought to pass up the promotion being offered you at work—and see how we react not only on the surface but on the deepest levels of our being.

THE DEEPER INTELLIGENCE MARKS BOUNDARIES

The constantly changing shadows caused by the intense but flickering light of the fireplace perfectly matched the ebb and flow of emotions palpable in the room. The mother and father listened to their fifteen-year-old son, Brad, speak convincingly about why he should be allowed to join a rock band made up of some friends in his school.

Brad insisted, "The band practices a lot, and no one in

the group uses drugs. It's just a group of guys who really like music and who are very creative. I won't get into any trouble. You've got to let go of me sometime."

The mother and father obviously were concerned about who their teenager son's friends were. Initially they were skeptical about the son's proposal. But Brad was as persuasive as a successful trial lawyer giving his closing argument. As the light glistened upon his long blond hair, with an occasional grin flashing between his pleading, both the mother and father yearned to give their son his heart's desire. Even though they had significant reservations about his being with an older crowd, he was basically well-behaved. And he was at an age when they sincerely wanted to encourage his independence and decision-making.

For several days the mother and father agonized over their decision. They sought counsel from older and supposedly wiser friends, who encouraged them to let their son make his own decision. Feeling caught in the all-too-familiar no-man's land where there don't seem to be any clear-cut rules, they reluctantly decided to let Brad join the band.

Feeling caught in the all-too-familiar no-man's land where there don't seem to be any clear-cut rules, they reluctantly decided to let Brad join the band.

It was only later that the father recalled his son's somewhat strange comment to him after they had discussed the issue again and granted his request. Brad had said, "I think I'm going to be sick. I just ate too much chocolate cake." The father thought it was a rather odd remark, because a good amount of time had passed since Brad had eaten. But at the moment Brad's father brushed the comment off as inconsequential.

A few months went by, and gradually it became clear that Brad could not handle the degree of freedom he had been given. His behavior deteriorated and his grades dropped. He became increasingly hostile and sullen. He neglected his household chores. He began coming home past his curfew. And he had started smoking, causing his parents to suspect he also might be experimenting with drugs.

The parents recognized they had a crisis on their hands—so they began to pull in the reins. In no uncertain terms, they told Brad they had been skeptical at the outset of his joining the band and hanging out with an older crowd. Now it was clear he just couldn't handle it.

Of course, Brad didn't take kindly to his parents' impingement on his freedom. But after the discussion (or battle, as it turned out) when his parents had reset the boundaries, Brad spontaneously made another of his seemingly inconsequential remarks: "Oh, did you hear about Roy Parnelli?" Brad said. "He just enlisted in the Army. He says he wants to get his life under control." Roy, whom Brad had admired years ago, had been in constant scrapes with the law since dropping out of high school.

Later that night, after some reflection on the exchange, Brad's father suddenly realized what his son was trying to tell them through his offhand remarks. The sequence suddenly made sense to him: First, there was a period of intense disagreement over where boundaries should be drawn (at the beginning of the rock band experience). Somewhat against their better judgement, he and his wife had loosened the boundaries. This was followed immediately by an offhand comment about being sick (a negative remark). Then, some time later, when the boundaries had been reset by his parents (at the conclusion of the rock band experience), Brad had shared a positive story about his friend Roy getting his life together in the Army.

In short, Brad was fighting with his parents over where his boundaries should be, and then indirectly thanking them for holding firm. The son was telling his parents that deep down he understood he was getting the discipline he needed. Through his remark about having eaten too much cake, he was saying in effect, "You've just given me too much freedom." When he added, "I'm going to get sick," he was virtually prophesying that there were going to be consequences for the excessive freedom.

Through his remark about having eaten too much cake, he was saying in effect, "You've just given me too much freedom."

In retrospect, this father realized two things. First, he was glad to know that pulling Brad out of the band was a good decision. But moreover, as he thought back to the initial too-much-cake remark, he distinctly recalled quickly pushing out of his mind a vague awareness—a restlessness—that dimly asked if anything had been overlooked in the decision. Brad's comment about the cake had registered briefly in his mind at the time, but he had quickly ignored the trigger and granted his son more freedom. Now that the father had more clearly identified a different trigger in a second situation (resetting firm boundaries had prompted a story about the benefit of strong boundaries), he had become a better listener and realized how he had overlooked an important message.

When proper and healthy boundaries were under threat

within this family, the deeper intelligence had known exactly what to do. And in spite of strong conscious feelings to the contrary, it had attempted to guide the persons involved—the father, the mother, and their son—toward the right decision.

Indeed, one of the unique functions of the deeper intelligence is its ability to know where the perfect boundaries are in our relationships. This function is extremely important, since much more often than we realize, various issues arise in our lives which have to do with setting and respecting boundaries.

I remember one patient, Louise, who was a particularly sensitive person and who'd had an especially difficult life. Louise was very likable and evoked strong urges in others to protect her. This included me. She also was working toward a degree in counseling, which gave us a some common ground that I often don't have with other patients.

One day, at the beginning of the therapy session, Louise made a casual request: "I'm taking a course and have to write a paper. I was wondering if I could borrow a book I've seen on your shelf. If you're not going to use it this week, I'll make sure I get it back to you at our next session. Even if you use it regularly, I could just stop by and borrow it for one or two days."

Before I'd known how to hear the deeper intelligence, I would have loaned her the book without a second thought. And she would have returned it to me a week or two later with a thank you, and her therapy would have rolled right along without any real importance given to the transaction. But I was just beginning to understand that another part of Louise—and of me—was very much alive. So I paused before answering to consider what input we could get from her deeper mind.

This was an awkward moment because examining such seemingly simple requests in light of the deeper intelligence often cuts against the grain of social kindness. So, after her request, I said somewhat apologetically, "Why don't we explore your request and see if it really is a good idea or not." I could tell Louise was hurt—and since she was quite self-critical, I knew she might feel she had imposed upon me. Or maybe she thought I was uncaring? Almost everything in me had wanted to say yes to Louise's request, but I knew it was in her best interest to try to listen to her deeper intelligence.

Louise became a little defensive. But almost immediately she started talking about her helpless aunt who was physically handicapped. "I know life is hard for her," she said, "but she really uses her disability at times to get other people to do things for her that she ought to do for herself."

Then Louise talked about the course—significantly on codependency—for which she was writing the paper. "In our class discussion, the subject of welfare came up. You wouldn't believe how some of my classmates can't see how dependent it makes the recipients," Louise observed.

Her deeper intelligence was speaking plainly, and the healthiest part of her mind was telling us: "Help me to be different from my aunt and my neighbor. Teach me the self-control and self-reliance my parents failed to instill."

Hmm. She has mentioned a helpless aunt who really isn't so helpless, taking advantage of others, and welfare recipients whose helplessness is being reinforced by the system. I hear a common theme of people not being inde-

45

pendent when they really ought to be. I was impressed that Louise's deeper mind seemed clearly to be addressing a boundary issue. I continued to listen. Finally she talked about her neighbors, who couldn't manage their own affairs and always borrowed things from everyone else in the neighborhood. These same neighbors tended to abuse alcohol and mismanage their money. She thought somebody should stand up to them and quit indulging them—that maybe some "tough love" would help them.

By this time, there was no question in my mind that deep down Louise knew where we should put the boundary regarding my loaning her a book. Louise consciously wanted to borrow a book, but her brilliant subconscious made its case that there was a greater reason not to loan her a book. The reason? Discipline and independence. Her deeper intelligence was speaking plainly, and the healthiest part of her mind was telling us: "Help me to be different from my aunt and my neighbor. Teach me the self-control and self-reliance my parents failed to instill. Teach me a better sense of where the boundaries go. Help me to be independent, not addictive or codependent. Help me not to violate your boundaries."

Through this seemingly inconsequential incident, Louise recognized a defect in herself and went on to correct the defect in her therapy. In a similar, subtle way, many times in everyday life people want us to help them set proper boundaries. Often they will test us to see if we are strong enough to help them build their own appropriate boundaries.

In both the situations mentioned—with Louise, and with the teenager, Brad—the major question was, "Where do the boundaries go?" Should the parents have allowed their son to join the rock band, or should they have blocked him? Should the therapist have allowed a patient to borrow a book, or should he have set a boundary that didn't allow the patient to use his personal possessions?

Obviously the deeper intelligence had a definite opinion

as to exactly where the boundaries should be set in both instances and had good reasons for doing so. But often the boundary mode's recommendations will surprise us. Yet once we understand the deeper intelligence's reasoning, we will marvel at its brilliance.

In Brad's situation, both he and his parents struggled over where to place the boundary, eventually setting it in the wrong place. Yet all along, his boundary mode knew what he needed and had already recommended where the boundary should be (through the cake remark)—yet no one "heard" or recognized its counsel. Brad had thought he needed freedom more than limits when, in fact, he still needed his parents to build control into him. In his own words, when he got too much freedom it made him sick—it deprived him of healthy functioning. Deep down Brad knew that he (and his parents) had been violating important boundaries of stability. If he had continued to live that way in an ongoing fashion, it truly would have meant death to his healthy side.

And when Louise seemingly made a harmless request to borrow a book, the boundary mode of her deeper intelligence commented with exceptional wisdom on why the request was actually harmful and not at all in her best interests. Louise, who consciously wanted to borrow a book, deep down knew she was violating the law of independence. And Brad knew the same.

* * *

The boundary mode teaches a great deal about the function of boundaries in our lives and why they are so important. First, it teaches that *boundaries give strength*. Generally speaking, if you are raised with reasonable but firm boundaries, eventually you will become a strong person. If you are raised with inadequate boundaries, you will become a weak person. This is why the absence of a parent can be so significant. There is no one there to build strength. Whenever you are weak, deep down you know it; and your deeper intelligence leads you to look for healing—for someone to build strong boundaries into you where you lack them.

The boundary mode teaches a great deal about the function of boundaries in our lives and why they are so important.

Clear boundaries are strong boundaries. They help you to define who you are and who you are not. My patient Louise was secretly asking me to show her where she started and where she ended. By refusing to lend her my book, I was saying to her, "This is who you are, and this is who I am. You are not an extension of me; you must manage life yourself."

Children do this throughout their development. Just as they frequently look in the mirror to see who they are, they test parents in numerous ways to make sure of who the parents are and, thus, who they are.

Yet, perhaps the most surprising insight that the boundary mode makes clear is that *deep down we all need exactly the same basic boundaries.* The reason for this is that in the depths of our being we have the same basic needs. One of those needs is for an unmistakable individuality; and, ironically, to be a true individual we require the strongest of boundaries.

When someone doesn't have the boundaries in place she needs, her deeper intelligence will hone in on her need until it is met—just as we saw happen with Brad and Louise.

THE DEEPER INTELLIGENCE PROVIDES STABILITY

It just doesn't get any easier, the father said to himself. *You would think that, after having already lost two children—one to hemophilia—I would be prepared for this. But I'm not.*

As his twenty-two-year-old son lay dying in the hospital bed next to his chair, his mind was almost numb from the pain. In the glow of the softly lit room, his son's steady breathing was all that could be heard.

It had been several hours since his son had even opened his eyes, and he grew weaker moment by moment. Only a few days ago he had been an active, vigorous young man, despite living daily with a life-threatening condition—hemophilia. Then it had happened—a skiing accident, internal bleeding, and now he was on the verge of leaving this world.

The father reflected on all the people who had stopped by—caring, well-meaning people. He had visited many of those same people in the past as their pastoral counselor, bringing comfort to them in their own crises. And as he had done with them, they had offered him words of comfort from favorite Scripture passages, remembrances of their own suffering, hope for the future, and offers to help in any way they could. But it was as if those words were a million miles away.

He wondered now if his words to them seemed as hollow as theirs did to him now in his own pain. *Where does the helper go for help? Where does the comforter go for comfort?* he pondered. He wasn't minimizing his spiritual needs, and he knew from experience he would find great comfort there eventually. But right now he didn't feel like praying or hearing any more seemingly empty words of comfort. The counselor was also a father in pain, and he didn't know where to turn.

Suddenly he felt a hand on his shoulder. He looked around to see the familiar face of a pediatrician who had attended his church for years. The physician's knowing look spoke volumes in the brief meeting of their eyes. The father wondered what his friend was going to say—perhaps another word of encouragement, or a question, or an observation about his son's very serious medical problem.

Yet the middle-aged doctor simply sat quietly beside him, occasionally glancing over at his friend, but mostly watching the young man continue to fight for his life. Eventually, after a long while—three quarters of an hour perhaps—the doctor stood up, once again placing his hand knowingly on the father's shoulder, revealed one last time an understanding look, and quietly walked out of the room.

Strangely, as the father sat in the room alone, he realized that without saying even one word his friend had helped him settle down. He felt strangely calmed after the wordless visit. His desperate thoughts cried out silently, *I wish I had realized how much his visit meant to me. I would have asked him to stay all night.* To this father, the short visit had been a great comfort.

Strangely, as the father sat in the room alone, he realized that without saying even one word his friend had helped him settle down.

This story reveals yet another important part of our deeper intelligence in action—the *stability mode*. Everyone needs to be emotionally held or supported by his environment and key figures in his life. The degree to which you have been stabilized, or held securely by those key figures, determines your basic internal stability. The stability you have received directly affects the development in your deeper mind of your stability mode, the part of you that attempts to contain a difficult situation without being overwhelmed. This part of you helps keep you in equilibrium no matter what happens.

Our stability mode is the most active part of us as it steadily holds us together, moment by moment. The deeper intelligence reveals just how crucial this mode is to us and how we desperately seek stability above all other needs.

While this mode may seem less important than the guidance or boundary modes (because it seems so quiet and in the background), it is not passive. Our stability mode is the most active part of us as it steadily holds us together, moment by moment. The deeper intelligence reveals just how crucial this mode is to us and how we desperately seek stability above all other needs. As I will make plain later, the stability mode is directly related to our first and most basic need in life—the need for commitment by at least one significant person to us. Throughout

51

our development we need someone to "hold" us so that we can work on getting our other needs met.

Just as the physician friend of the dying boy's father offered help with his silent show of strength and support, at times everyone needs to shore up their own or another's stability mode. The benefit the father derived from the pediatrician's visit teaches us again how we never stop identifying with those around us throughout our lives.

D. W. Winnicott was a famous British psychiatrist who had initially been a pediatrician. Winnicott coined the phrase "maternal hold," which became a well-known psychiatric term used to describe the basic security a person experiences in childhood from the most important early figure in his life, his mother.[3] I believe that, in essence, Winnicott was describing the mother's stability mode.

The importance of the stability mode is also related to one form of a famous medical syndrome seen in children known as the "Failure-to-Thrive Syndrome." Children with no apparent medical condition gradually suffer a decline in health, and many eventually die, because of a complete lack of physical contact or holding. This same need for holding or stabilizing continues throughout one's life. Statistics show that married people live longer, due in part probably because each person's stability mode strengthens the other person.

The stability mode comes into play also in raising children. In homes where two parents are present, and particularly in those where conflict is minimal, children are exposed to two strong stability modes instead of one. (Statistically, children with two-parent homes are better off emotionally.) The familiar television commercial in which the comforting father figure announces, "You're in good hands with Allstate," typifies the stability mode. If you have been in good hands—secure hands—then your stability mode will reflect that strength. And in turn, you will be able to provide "good hands" for someone else.

SOMETIMES MORE IS LESS

A friend told me a story about an informal support group for married couples he and his wife had joined. Prior to joining the group, he had recognized a tendency in himself to say too much and become involved too quickly, trying to "fix" other people. When he didn't know what to do, his motto was, "Say something," or, "Do something"—which generally meant taking over for others. However, the group had a very healthy rule: "No fixing allowed." They permitted only listening and sharing one's own experiences at appropriate moments. My friend was amazed at the growth that often followed, without lots of advice and "rescuing."

This same idea of "less is more" frequently occurs in virtually all of our relationships at certain moments. One of the biggest mistakes parents make is to try to do too much for their young adults. More growth occurs in adolescents when, for example, they are given consequences for failing to carry out chores rather than when they are repeatedly reminded of their forgotten chores. And, too often parents who watch their adolescent come and go without saying much believe they are not doing much for their teenager when, in fact, they are giving him exactly what the situation calls for.

This same idea of "less is more" frequently occurs in virtually all of our relationships at certain moments.

Strength is at the heart of the stability mode. Certainly we have different needs at different times as human beings; we need to know when to be flexible and when to be firm. The stability mode is always interested in being as strong as possible to be able to face any challenge. And we should be prepared to be as strong as a situation calls for. But in each situation, we have to rethink what real strength is.

Many successful people have well-developed stability modes. John Wooden was perhaps the most successful coach in the history of sports. His basketball teams at U.C.L.A. won ten national championships in twelve years, a record unmatched in any sport, especially considering his level of competition. While Wooden had many gifts as a coach, the trait that stood out more than any to me was his incredible stability. No matter how difficult things became for his team, he always came across like a Rock of Gibraltar. I can still see him sitting in the heat of the battle when things were going against his team—his arms folded, his eyes observing everything—just as poised as when he was ahead by twenty points. At a time when most coaches (particularly basketball coaches) would be openly distraught, Wooden was in control. His teams played the same way he behaved, rarely losing their poise.

General Colin Powell reminds himself every day of the need to reinforce his own stability mode. He keeps on his desk a quote from the ancient Greek philosopher Thucydides, "Nothing impresses men like restraint." Powell is reminding himself that sometimes less is more—that is, less overt self-expressiveness is often more powerful. Obviously, Powell developed a magnificent stability mode to rise to the top of his profession as Chairman of the Joint Chiefs of Staff.

Not only does the stability mode in us express its strength by demonstrating self-control over our emotions; it also comes into play when we must deal with the emotions of others. A strong stability mode reflects an inordinate capacity to "contain" the emotions of others without being overwhelmed ourselves. One of the great challenges for our stability mode is to be able to literally hold or contain the powerful emotions of others without reacting in a similar way. At these moments, it is helpful to think of ourselves as a container for the emotions of others who "dump" into us.

In essence, her child, with outbursts of different sorts, says to her, "See what you can do with these emotions— show me how to handle this!"

Many times, for example, a mother must contain the powerful emotions of her child. When the mother is able to do this without being overwhelmed, she models in a powerful way how to handle painful emotions. In essence, her child, with outbursts of different sorts, says to her, "See what you can do with these emotions—show me how to handle this!" The strength of that mother's stability mode will determine her ability to contain her child's powerfully unpleasant emotional states.

This need to serve as a "container" for the powerful emotions of others continues throughout our lifetime. Others may attempt through various maneuvers (many indirect) to make us feel what they feel. For example, a person who is guilt-ridden may try to make you feel guilty over a certain matter. How you handle that kind of powerful emotion may be very important in the life of that person. Instead of being overwhelmed and retaliating in a hostile, guilt-inducing manner, you may be able to make your point that you are not guilty without being overwhelmed. When you do this, you have demonstrated a very healthy stability mode.

The very first thing every patient who walks in my door says to me indirectly is, "Fix my stability mode—make it stronger."

As a result of being exposed to the deeper intelligence of each of my patients, I now understand that there is an "invisible shield" of stability around each person. Many times this shield of protection has holes in it and is breaking down. The very first thing every patient who walks in my door says to me indirectly is, "Fix my stability mode—make it stronger." Of course, patients don't know this. Yet, nevertheless, they repeatedly are saying to me, "Before anything else gets clarified, make sure this relationship is stable. I want the commitment, the privacy, and the freedom from intrusion that gives me strength."

This is the first part of the patient's mind I can address—and my patients give me an incredible permission to build into their stability mode. How I behave determines whether their stability mode becomes weaker or stronger.

This reminds me of a patient, Fran, who had repeatedly been manipulated and controlled by others. Once Fran was silent an entire session, and I debated (the entire session) whether or not to intervene with even a simple question or encouragement to talk. However, because she had built trust in me and because of her strong inclination to seek out people who controlled her, I decided to wait on her to talk. When the session ended with neither one of us saying a word (except hello and good-bye), I wasn't sure I had done the right thing. But I knew I would find out in a week.

The following session, Fran showed up in an upbeat

56

mood, never mentioned her silence or mine directly, and repeatedly talked about helpful people—including professionals—who brought calm to difficult situations. Thus, her deeper intelligence confirmed my decision and taught me in a fresh way how important good basic holding is in a relationship. During that session of mutual silence, Fran had needed—more than she needed anything else—for me to build strength into her by remaining self-contained.

The same invisible shield of stability that surrounds a person in psychotherapy is present, of course, in everyday life. This means that we have the ability to strengthen or weaken every person we meet. The closer we are to someone, the more powerfully we affect their stability mode. This is why sexual abuse, particularly at an early age when the stabilizing shield is in its infancy, is so devastating. At that moment an adult has damaged in untold ways the stabilizing shield of his young victim. This invisible shield can remain damaged for years and may be reflected in a lifetime of instability. Of course, there are other ways of damaging the protective shield a person possesses. The loss of a parent at an early age can have similar effects. (No one, in fact, has escaped *some* damage to his stabilizing shield.)

Because of our vulnerability to each other, this means we have an incredible responsibility toward one another. To truly make our neighbor stronger, which is the essence of love, we must respect his or her deepest needs. To truly respect our neighbor means we must understand what his deepest needs are, or else we could do severe damage to his stability mode, his shield of stability, and not know it. We must know these needs—in short, the "rules" we live by—to know what strengthens the stability mode and what undermines it.

* * *

If you can begin to grasp these three functions of your deeper intelligence, you will begin to learn how to hear the deeper intelligence. First, you must keep in mind that we all have a hidden but remarkably perceptive deeper intelligence that is phenomenally alert and could be speaking at any moment. If you realize that everyone's deeper intelligence above all seeks stability, that will help you to hear its messages.

Also you should ask yourself at various times in different relationships where the boundaries are. Try to get a sense of what boundaries really are. There are plenty of times in life where we share life together—laughing, working on a task, family or community activities—and it seems like there are no boundaries or boundaries aren't important. And yet it is still important to think about where the boundaries are, for they are always there and greatly concern the deeper intelligence. Many times people are crossing boundaries without realizing it, for example, moving from being good friends into people attempting to control others.

In a few chapters I will address the three basic needs the deeper intelligence reveals that we have. Once you add this to your understanding, you should be much more attune to your deeper intelligence. I will also clarify some other important issues in one-to-one relationships, which will help you spot common ways we fight the deeper intelligence.

CHAPTER FOUR

Roadblocks to Progress

"O, would some power the gift give us to see
ourselves as others see us."
"To a Louise"
Robert Burns

If we truly are to know ourselves and appreciate the great mind we have been given, we first must know that for several major reasons we have a tendency to hide part of ourselves from our conscious awareness. Often what is hidden is reality or the truth, and what seems more "real," i.e., our conscious awareness, in actuality may be feelings that are notoriously fickle and do not reflect the wisdom of the deeper mind. If we can recognize when we are hiding, we can learn how to look harder and more realistically at our true selves and overcome roadblocks to growth.

A few years ago I had a unique experience with a Hollywood celebrity, which reveals much about how our mind works—particularly when it comes to handling strong issues. This man had read a previous book of mine that focused in part on the importance of a healthy spirituality in our lives.[1] It intrigued him, so he called me and over a few months he and I had several interesting discussions via telephone. We began a friendship of sorts, and finally, he invited me to meet him in person whenever I was in California.

I did just that during a trip to the West Coast for a speaking engagement. As I drove to his home near the beach on a bright October afternoon, I was very much looking forward to the meeting. Yet, as I approached his house I also felt uneasy. I wondered if we would hit it off in person, as we had on the phone, or whether we might run out of things to talk about. Would we like each other or be disappointed?

All of this was a blur in my mind as I rang the doorbell— then suddenly this well-known person was standing face-to-face before me and inviting me into his surprisingly modest home. There was a natural uncertainty between us as we walked slowly down the entrance hall into his living room, exchanging chitchat. I was somewhat re-lieved to see he also seemed a little anxious.

As we continued talking, slowly warming up to each other, a beautiful Himalayan cat appeared in the doorway. It stood there regally, surveying the scene—which prob-ably most noticeably to her included me, a stranger to her domain. There was a slight pause in our conversation as I beheld the cat.

Suddenly my friend counseled me, "Let her come to you. She'll decide when she wants to approach you." A few moments later, the cat jumped elegantly into a chair and plopped herself down. As we talked, she continued to observe her surroundings with caution.

It was several hours later in our visit that the signifi-cance of my host's remark sank in. His seemingly casual comment about how to approach his cat (or rather, how not to approach her) was actually a coded message I believe he wanted to get across to me: *Let me approach you when I feel comfortable in doing so. You have definite spiritual convictions, I do not. I'm cautious and wary, just like my cat. I want to get to know you and the spiritual convictions you hold, but I must go slowly. And I want you to do the same.*

My conscious mind had missed this at first—but my

deeper mind had picked up his meaning. At the time, however, the only thing I was consciously aware of was a feeling—a strong intuition that I needed to proceed very gently no matter what we discussed.

My new friend also gave me another clue: He mentioned that he had suffered heart trouble in the last year. I realized then that this was one of the reasons he had wanted to talk to me. He had had his first serious brush with death, and that had caused him to consider his eventual and eternal destiny.

During our time together that afternoon, I began to introduce the serious subjects I felt he would be interested in. But I did so in a very general sense—talking about other people, keeping the subject away from anything personal unless he led the way. In essence, I did what he had asked me to do, through his remark about his cat: I let him come to me.

We must appreciate in a new way how often our feelings are disassociated from important information we are communicating. If we understand the limitation of our conscious feelings, we will be able to hear our own mind's voice. My celebrity friend was, I am sure, unaware of any significant conscious feeling telling him to make sure I proceeded slowly so that I could be of help to him. Yet his deeper mind appreciated in a heartbeat how anxious he was about a topic we were going to discuss.

In a day that stresses messages like "search your heart, go with your gut, trust your feelings," we must recognize that these messages basically ignore the right brain and encourage us to focus exclusively on our limited, conscious, left-brain feelings. Sometimes gut feelings or intuition can be helpful and are linked to the deeper intelligence; but more often they give us very limited information about what is truly going on in our "guts." We need right-brain knowledge, and not just left-brain feelings, to know all of ourselves and to make our best decisions.

In this chapter I want to show you how limited our

immediate feelings are—but, when combined with right-brain input, how they can be very helpful in self-understanding. This is the great lesson the deeper intelligence itself attempts to teach us. Every person who consults me—whether he knows it or not, and most don't—does so deep down in order to understand his deeper intelligence, to see past his immediate and superficial feelings.

If we are going to hear our deeper intelligence and penetrate to the heart of its many messages for us, we must begin to know where our conscious selves end and understand how limited our immediate feelings can be. When we do that, we will be better spouses, better parents, better friends, better bosses, better employees (and better therapists).

If we are going to hear our deeper intelligence and penetrate to the heart of its many messages for us, we must begin to know where our conscious selves end and understand how limited our immediate feelings can be.

THE MASKS OF SUPPRESSION AND REPRESSION

We all wear masks that we aren't even conscious of wearing. In the case I related earlier of the mother whose son had just died of leukemia, I witnessed one of those masks with real clarity and encountered face-to-face the crucial distinction between the two ways we handle overwhelming pain, guilt, and fear: *suppression* and *repression*.

Suppression means a conscious blocking of something from our awareness. Yet we can bring it into our awareness anytime we want. For example, we can recall a childhood experience at will, even though we may not be thinking about it at the time. *Repression*, on the other hand, entails a complete blocking of certain experiences from our conscious awareness. It is, in fact, unconscious blocking, in the sense that we don't know we're blocking it. It is one of the most striking attributes we possess as human beings, and is, I believe, *the most under-appreciated aspect to our mental makeup*.

The woman who had just lost her son demonstrated the phenomenon of repression by not accepting the reality that her son had died. Of course, she heard my words—but the reality of her son's death was too powerful for her to withstand at the moment. She had no awareness she was blocking reality at the time; she simply had to hide her overwhelming grief from herself. It was something she had no immediate choice over; her mind simply took over in a protective way. No matter who we are we have all repressed a number of experiences.

This fact, that we cannot directly access the unconscious mind where our hidden self lies, is not well understood by many therapists who frequently confuse suppression and repression. They fail to see the importance of distinguishing between the two, and mistakenly refer to both with the often-used term *denial*.

Denial is a popular term we repeatedly hear, particularly among professionals in the recovery movement and those dealing with codependency. Over and over we hear the phrase, "He/she is in denial." Many therapists attempt to deal with denial through repeated confrontation, viewing the patient as someone who is consciously lying to himself. While this works at times with a problem like substance abuse (because the destructive potential of addiction is so great a person simply can't go on denying it), this technique of forcing information out of the deeper mind does not work with most other issues.

True denial is completely unconscious; it essentially is the same thing as repression. As a therapist I must understand and realize that I can't force information out of a person that he is unconsciously blocking out. I have to know my way around the blocks.

It's also impossible to reveal the secrets of the deeper mind by asking direct questions. The deeper intelligence itself is the way around the blocks—around denial or repression—and where the real insight is. The deeper mind wants to communicate to us what we don't know. But for patients who have not been helped to hear their deeper intelligence, the result is often limited self-understanding, bad decision-making, and continued suffering. Only memories and experiences that are *suppressed* are available to immediate recall by posing to our minds a direct question. Events that are *repressed* have to be accessed by other means; we must approach our deeper mind on its terms.

Recently, repressed memories have come into the forefront of public attention, particularly in relation to people who during therapy are "discovering they were sexually or physically abused." Many have rightly questioned the techniques of certain therapists who have been accused of planting ideas in patient's minds. It is indeed very easy for a therapist to produce false memories of abuse in a patient. Any therapist who introduces the idea of sexual or physical abuse has planted an idea in the patient's mind.

The deeper intelligence clearly teaches that there is one way for a therapist to accurately uncover memories, and that is by letting the deeper intelligence go first. In other words, a therapist should never go ahead of a patient but simply provide an environment where proper uncovering of memories can occur. Spontaneously, the deeper intelligence will do so. This relates to the guidance function of the deeper intelligence. Under the right conditions, the deeper intelligence longs to reveal its secrets.

PLAN A VERSUS PLAN B

We often have an unstated agenda—a "plan B"—to go with our stated objective, or "plan A." Let me give you an example from a therapy session.

It involved a patient named Marge who at the beginning of a session made a seemingly simple request: "Dr. Hodges, before I forget, would you please hold the check I'm going to give you today for three days until I get paid?" Certainly, to almost anyone's left brain, Marge's request would have seemed a minor and innocent one. She appeared honest, straightforward, and intent on paying her bill.

But now, having become a true detective of the mind, I waited and pondered before making a reply. And I had a marvelous opportunity to study the reality that was on *both* levels of Marge's mind—because I saw her simple wish to slightly modify our normal financial agreement as a trigger or *reality event*. My basic thought was, *Does Marge's right brain—her deeper intelligence—agree with her left brain on the true meaning of her request?* In other words: *Is her request insignificant as far as the deeper mind sees it? Or is there a broader reality that makes more sense?* The wonderful thing for a therapist when a question like this comes up is that you can virtually always get an answer for it—from the deeper intelligence.

One of the most important factors in getting to know the deeper intelligence is to *give it an opportunity to speak.* The best way to accomplish this as a therapist is simply to stay out of its way—to just let it communicate. I merely ask the patient to keep talking, keep exploring until I can put something together. I have only one request: "Say exactly where your thoughts go so that I can hear you think. Try not to screen anything that comes up." I have learned that the deeper intelligence is far more capable and desirous of revealing valuable information than I had ever dreamed.

This technique of encouraging the patient's thoughts to lead the way is loosely called "free association." It originated with Freud, although he himself did not appreciate the gold he was mining with his very own idea. This technique is mostly out of favor today, but that is only because therapists didn't know how to properly use it back when that's all they had (i.e., before the discovery of the deeper intelligence). It will be one of the cornerstones of the therapy of the future because it is the primary road to the deeper intelligence. Also, among those therapists who claim to use the technique, far too many often really don't—they interrupt and get in the way by injecting too many directives into therapy. Or like Freud, they simply fail to hear the messages from the deeper mind. The essence of free association is that a person truly faces himself as he reveals how he thinks, by giving his brilliantly perceptive deeper intelligence a chance to speak.

The problem with many patients is that often they don't *want* to hear from the deeper intelligence. This was the case with Marge—at first. She immediately pressed me for an answer to her question about my holding her check. But I refrained from answering and simply asked her to keep talking. In essence, I was saying to her, "I'm not making a decision without hearing from your deeper intelligence. I want to see if this request means anything to your right brain."

Not long after that, Marge started talking about an aunt "who has a back problem and has exploited it to get on welfare." *Hmm, she's telling me about someone who's taking unfair advantage of the system,* I thought. Later, I almost couldn't believe it when she told me about a friend who "has a problem telling the truth, which has gotten her into a lot of trouble. Her attorney knows it, and he accepted a bad check from her. He should have given it back to her and never accepted it in the first place." *Wow!* I thought. *That's a pretty obvious parallel case.*

Then she spontaneously went on to talk about addictions of various types—about people who live off of others and who can't complete tasks. *The evidence is beginning to pile up,* I said to myself.

At that point I was certain what her deeper intelligence was revealing to me: Granting her extra time to pay her bill meant she would be living off of me—as if she were someone who exploited welfare or took advantage of other people. In other words, I could see what one reality event—delaying payment of her bill—meant to her on the surface and also what it meant on the deeper level of her mind—that such actions are wrong. What began as a harmless proposal to Marge's left brain had another, far more powerful and negative meaning to the rest of her mind. Even though I would be holding the check for just three days, those three days were crucial. In essence they were a test from Marge's deeper intelligence: "Are you going to help me recognize and control an unhealthy part of myself?"

Once I reflected on Marge's other problems, I could see how much sense the deeper intelligence was making. She'd been addicted to pain medication, she found it difficult to complete tasks, and she had to deal with the depression that came with her failures.

If I had granted her the favor, I would have robbed her of the independence she so desperately needed.

The true meaning of Marge's request for a favor regarding her check was that by asking this, she was trying to learn better ways of coping with life. If I had granted her the favor, I would have robbed her of the independence she so desperately needed. Deep down, Marge was requesting that I not accept her bad check and wait until she could actually live up to her financial commitment. Marge knew she was weak when it came to living within clear boundaries and living up to commitments. She really wanted me to accept her check only when it was good—and to communicate to her that I understood what she really needed. She was *indirectly* asking me to help her change by refusing her request. So that's exactly what I did. If I had not known how to listen to the deeper intelligence, however, I would easily have missed an opportunity to help her grow.

Learning to listen to the deeper intelligence first and foremost means *listening* rather than *feeling*. This is the fundamental insight necessary if we are to hear the deeper intelligence. So often in therapy, particularly at first, before a person has caught on to some degree how the mind works, when I point out to her what the deeper intelligence is clearly saying, a patient's immediate response often is, "Oh, I don't feel that." The point is, of course, that *we don't feel* what our deeper mind is trying to tell us. This is often a very difficult thing to accept, because we are so accustomed to operating on our feelings.

The point is, of course, that we don't feel what our deeper mind is trying to tell us.

For example, in Marge's case, if she had not understood how her mind worked, she easily could have denied that she was telling me not to hold her check despite the fact that her deeper intelligence communication was crystal clear. This is the great disconnection in ourselves which we must learn to appreciate, a disconnection our deeper intelligence attempts to overcome.

To make the best decisions, we must listen for right-brain input—or "Plan B"—which is ruled by insight and understanding, in order to round out our left-brain input—or "Plan A"—which is essentially feelings-dominated and therefore severely limited in its utility.

As we recall a number of the stories of individuals I have told in this book, we see how limited their feelings often were. My patient Marge thought it was a good idea to ask me to hold her check—but it wasn't. A grieving lady thought her son was alive even after being presented with the fact of his death. Dr. Langs's patient, Sally, thought it would be good to bring her husband into her therapy when clearly it wasn't. Although nightmares tried to warn my friend that accepting a lucrative business opportunity wasn't a good idea, he thought it was—but it proved disastrous. My celebrity friend did not recognize two major motivations in his life: a powerful search for meaning and his eternal destiny and the fear of talking about both.

Throughout this book we will repeatedly see how people tend to develop a Plan A when deep down they desperately want Plan B. And I hope you will start to recognize in others and in yourself when the same thing occurs.

The fact that frequently over a single issue we have one plan from our left brain and one plan from our right brain means that we each have two different value systems struggling within ourselves. By paying close attention to these two value systems in a multitude of situations (such as those I've just mentioned), we come to some striking conclusions: Our left brain values are highly individualistic, varying form person to person, but our right brain values are consistently the same (based on our three primary needs, as we will see in chapter 5).

The fact that frequently over a single issue we have one plan from our left brain and one plan from our right brain means that we each have two different value systems struggling within ourselves.

For example, some people will feel (the left-brain influence) that I should have held Marge's check, while others wouldn't agree. However, deep down if we could access everyone's right brain just as can be done in therapy, everyone would agree that Marge should not have been given a break concerning her check.

I say this with confidence because I literally have observed hundreds of similar situations, and the right-brained deeper intelligence has been perfectly consistent in declaring its needs. Once we comprehend the crucial fact that two different value systems are at work within us, our self understanding increases dramatically. Then false differences of opinion (with ourselves or others), which are incredibly common, can be seen for what they are. The fact that our feelings are virtually always limited to our left brain is what makes it so difficult to consider that we may have a difference of opinion about a matter within our very own selves.

The breakthrough to the deeper mind is a breakthrough to the deepest part of our mind, to the deepest and strongest motivations that we possess. Now with great clarity we are able to distinguish between the superficial, pseudo-motivations of our left brain and the real motivations of our right brain. In essence, this discovery means that we

70

have broken through to the motivation center of our minds, what for years has been referred to as our "heart."

The breakthrough to the deeper mind is a breakthrough to the deepest part of our mind, to the deepest and strongest motivations that we possess.

GATEWAY VIRTUES: INTEGRITY AND HUMILITY

As we seek to know ourselves, to find our true selves, the deeper intelligence speaks loudly and clearly as to what is required of us. Above all, to enter into this new awareness we need integrity and humility. By integrity I mean such a love for the truth that it colors everything we do. And truth is closely linked to humility. The truth about ourselves—how limited our conscious minds are, how prone we are to self-deception—compels us to develop humility. Cultivating a humility which causes us to recognize the limitations of our highly cherished feelings will help us enormously. I'm speaking of a humility that allows us to say to ourselves, "My feelings, no matter how strong, possess a great capacity to lie to me, to give me limited information about who I really am and what I should do."

Only humility enables us to undercut the false pride that often accompanies our feelings. We must in some way be like Socrates, who once said he was the smartest man in Athens because he realized that he didn't know very much—while the rest of the so-called wise men of his day thought they knew a great deal.

71

ROADBLOCK TO PROGRESS

It had been a long time since I'd felt this helpless as a therapist. I had watched my patient, JoAnna, go steadily downhill during the last month, becoming progressively more negative and self-critical. She told me, "I'm beginning to think my ex-husband was right. He said I can't do anything right."

JoAnna, a divorcee in her early thirties, had been in therapy for a year. Until recently she had made slow but significant gains and was beginning to make better choices in her relationships, particularly with men. But now, as she continued her recent slide downhill, one thought kept going through my mind: *This is so puzzling. She has been doing so well and now she is back into her old thought patterns for some reason.* I had no idea what was causing it. Nothing major had changed in her life, other than that she seemed to be talking more about her relationship with her critical parents.

This is so puzzling. She has been doing so well and now she is back into her old thought patterns for some reason. I had no idea what was causing it.

I even considered a new trial of anti-depressant medication, but JoAnna had had the full spectrum of anti-depressants before she had come to me, none of which had helped and all of which caused her very unpleasant side effects. Psychotherapy had helped her when nothing else had, but now it seemed to have lost its power.

At this point in my career I was a fairly experienced

therapist. I knew how to listen to the deeper intelligence, or thought I did, and I had seen its power. But for once it seemed to be letting me down. No matter what I said, JoAnna seemed to get worse.

Then one day JoAnna, who was a supervisor, described one of her subordinates as someone "who was never satisfied with himself. No matter what I do, I can't seem to reach him," she said.

When I heard that comment, at a time of frustration in trying everything I knew to do to help her, it dawned on me that JoAnna was probably describing herself. She had been so criticized as a child, raised by such perfectionist parents, that she was simply doing a number on herself. *That must explain it,* I thought in a brief moment of relief. *She is really punishing herself.*

It was not an uncommon conclusion I had come to—that the reason JoAnna wasn't improving was that she was just a self-defeating patient. Difficult patients are the subject of much discussion among therapists, and patients like JoAnna are described in colloquial terms as "martyrs." Yet, although I partly had concluded that JoAnna was a martyr and thus was causing her own suffering, I wasn't totally convinced.

I had one last option: I could obtain a second opinion from a colleague. Perhaps someone else had a better way of helping these negativistic, self-punishing patients. In addition, I could have a blind spot and be overlooking something the patient was trying to tell me. So I presented the case to Dr. Langs, whom I had been working with from time to time in supervision of my cases.

After he had quietly listened to me present verbatim notes of a recent session with JoAnna, he simply said, "You're really murdering your patient, aren't you?"

I will never forget those words. Dr. Langs knew me well enough to be that blunt. And I knew him well enough to know that he was almost always right when it came to helping me and other therapists see our blind spots. And he was right. I saw that when JoAnna had been talking about her subordinate who was never satisfied with his performance, her deeper intelligence was clearly talking about *me*—yet I couldn't hear it. As I came to see, very subtly I had been criticizing her in my comments—comments such as, "You seem to be saying things are worse because you're excessively blaming yourself." In other words I was blaming the patient for not getting better, implying that she could do something about it.

With Dr. Langs's help, over the next few weeks I made some subtle but effective changes in how I approached JoAnna. The turnaround was amazing. In fact, dramatic improvement occurred, including the surfacing of key issues which JoAnna had not been able to deal with because my secret criticism had been overshadowing everything else.

I had experienced what another of my professors had called a "King David Reaction." You may recall the story from the Old Testament. David was the reigning king of Israel. He had an affair with Bathsheba, the beautiful wife of one of his devoted soldiers, impregnated her, and then had the soldier murdered to cover it all up. This happened despite the fact that David had had many concubines.

The prophet Nathan was instructed by God to confront David with his sin, and he did so by telling David a parable in disguise. He reported to the king that there was a wealthy farmer in Israel who had hundreds of cattle, and yet he had stolen his neighbor's only cow and then murdered the neighbor. Upon hearing the story, David became enraged and demanded that Nathan have the man brought to him immediately. Nathan replied, "David, that man is you!"[2]

In some way I know a bit of what King David must have felt when I'd thought the problem was with my patient— yet it actually was with me.

THE EXTERNALIZING MODE

The phenomenal ability we have to see in others our own shortcomings without seeing them in ourselves is a process in our deeper minds called the *externalizing mode*. The externalizing mode takes that which we find uncomfortable about ourselves and attempts to make it "external." I attempted to place my own failure on my patient just as King David was willing to place his failure on a farmer. In short, the externalizing mode of the deeper mind is the part of us that wants to attribute our negative traits to others, to give others responsibility for what is our responsibility. It plays "the blame game." We all externalize, and we do it a lot more than we think we do—several times a day. (As we'll see in chapter 11, externalization is intricately linked to codependency.)

In short, the externalizing mode of the deeper mind is the part of us that wants to attribute our negative traits to others, to give others responsibility for what is our responsibility.

The universal tendency to externalize is what Mark Twain referred to when he said the town drunk is an elected office. In other words, everyone in the town has a vested interest in locating failure outside of themselves; we all tend to scapegoat someone. Scapegoats are a natural occurrence wherever we look—in families, in businesses, on athletic teams.

The need to externalize arises because we desire to be free of any faults. "To err" may be human, but it doesn't mean we like it. We desire to be whole. Unfortunately, the reality is that we all are far from perfect. Because of this dilemma—the wish for perfection and the failure to attain it—we all too frequently resort to the externalizing mode.

Once a friend of mine clearly revealed his own externalizing mode while we were playing together on a softball team. That summer he frequently berated a famous professional baseball player for being egotistical because the player was always quoting his own statistics. However, several times during our softball season, my friend himself would quickly correct our teammates who made inaccurate comments about *his* statistics. I remember one night a teammate said to my friend, "Frank, you had a great game last week—two home runs and five RBIs."

All around us we find people who can't see themselves except in the mirror of their neighbor.

Frank quickly corrected him that he had had *seven* RBIs, clearly revealing he was also preoccupied with his own statistics. All around us we find people who can't see themselves except in the mirror of their neighbor.

While we may think the externalizing mode is necessary for us to cope, it is actually an unhealthy part of us. In truth, the externalizing mode wants others to suffer in our place; it wants others to carry the pain only we should carry. It is one thing to allow a friend to comfort you in pain and to share your frustrations with you; but it is another to impose that on someone who is unwilling. And we pay a high price for playing the blame game through the externalizing mode: alienation from our neighbor because we blame him, loss of self-respect, and in the end a lack of integrity or wholeness.

In contrast to the deeper intelligence and its three core modes, which emphasize healing, truth, and growth, the externalizing mode is a major part of what I have referred to as the punishing intelligence. When we heed its voice, we end up being punished. It is the primary cause of disturbances and destruction in many types of relationships. Problems between parents and children, conflicts on the job between a manager and employee—all are often exacerbated by our devious externalizing mode. We can never underestimate its duplicitous power.

In summary, we have two parts to our great hidden intelligence—a limited punishing intelligence and a wiser deeper intelligence.

Time after time, patients subconsciously enter psychotherapy not to be healed but to perpetuate a deviant pattern of externalizing their pain. Unknowingly, my patients want me to join with them in this covert enterprise, a secret plan that tarnishes them—and me—if I play into their game. The only antidote to the almost overwhelming tendency of the punishing intelligence is to follow the guidance of the deeper intelligence. At all times the deeper intelligence is aware of the tricks of the externalizing mode, and at key moments it will attempt to call our attention to the externalizing mode in order to bring about true healing. In summary, we have two parts to our great hidden intelligence—a limited punishing intelligence and a wiser deeper intelligence. From the depths of our being, there is an ongoing battle between the two. Indeed, the deeper intelligence attempts to *deliver us* from the punishing intelligence.

Recognition of the destructive externalizing mode is not a recent event. Jesus identified the universal human tendency to constantly find fault with our neighbor and the high price we pay for such a maneuver. He said, "Why do you look at the speck in your brother's eye, but do not consider the plank in your own eye? . . . First remove the plank from your own eye, and then you will see clearly to remove the speck from your brother's eye," (Matt. 7:3, 5 NKJV).

Almost two thousand years later, Sigmund Freud drew our attention to one of the simple tricks of the mind, something he called projection. Projection means we attribute to others faults or traits that we possess in an attempt to rid ourselves of them. Just as someone projects a photographic slide onto a screen, we project our faults onto others. This is the same thing as externalization.

It is striking that these remarkably similar observations on externalization have gone largely overlooked—by both the church and society in general. Certainly one major reason for this is that the conclusions hit too close to home. Jesus and Freud both hold a mirror up for us to see ourselves, and we don't like what we see. And when we don't like what we see, we often simply deny it. As they both suggested, denial is first cousin to externalization.

If we truly want to know ourselves, we must take this wisdom on externalizing behavior seriously. Robert Langs did in the school of psychotherapy he founded. He insisted that therapists should take every word out of their patients' mouths as potentially applying to the therapist. Langs taught that no matter who a patient talks about—a friend, himself, his father, anyone—the therapist should pay attention to what the patient says about that person, and then ask a simple question: Could my patient's deeper intelligence be talking about me?[3]

This is a wonderful starting point for all our relationships. We must begin to consider that every word out of our mouths could be a description of a part of ourselves we just don't recognize. If we adopt this attitude, we will begin to develop a genuine humility that will bring a breath of fresh air to all our dealing with others. When this occurs, once in a while we each will have a King David reaction that we eventually recognize, and then we will truly begin to know ourselves.

The principle here is never underestimate our ability to hide from ourselves. Just because we don't feel we are doing or saying something doesn't mean that is the case. We are remarkably capable of delivering a message and then denying that fact. There is enormous benefit in appreciating how great the potential for denial is in our communications. Then if a spouse, boss, or even one of our children confront us about a particular communication we are unaware of having made and don't immediately feel, we might be more inclined to listen instead of reflexively denying even the remotest of possibilities they could be right.

As one professor of mine once told a group of residents during my training in psychiatry, "If you don't remember anything else I teach you, remember how often we project our feelings on to others."

OVERCOMING ROADBLOCKS TO GROWTH

If it is true that our feelings are far more limited than we've thought and that we often have a far better plan operating in the back of our minds than what our left-brain informational system is giving us, then imagine where this leads us. Imagine what kind of revolution in self-knowledge and quality of life we could experience. Feelings have the possibility of being put in their proper place and no longer allowed to be our lord and master, wreaking havoc in our lives: marriages trashed, children abused, jobs lost, and more.

At this point, you may be tempted to think the work of knowing the deeper intelligence is too difficult and simply want to throw up your hands. Or you may think you don't have the ability to look so deeply at yourself. But just because our capacity to fool ourselves is great doesn't mean we can't know ourselves. In fact, if our capacity to fool ourselves is great, then we must be even more aware and demand more of ourselves in order to know ourselves.

I have good news! Even though we have this malignant capacity to mislead ourselves and others, we also have the passageway to the deeper intelligence. We have discovered our right brain—the deepest part of ourselves. It provides enormous insight in helping us learn who we really are.

If we can start with an acute awareness of the limitations of our conscious mind including our conscious feelings, we will be well ahead of most. This awareness will leave us ready to hear new information from our deeper intelligence.

The challenge in facing our deeper intelligence is to recognize the moments when it is making a clear-cut appearance and then to make an accurate interpretation. In the meantime, there is plenty of wisdom it has already imparted to us, which can greatly benefit us as we walk through life, day by day.

PART TWO

The
Deeper Intelligence
at Work

Our Three Core Needs

There is nothing quite like the excitement of the impending birth of a new child. That's true particularly if you already have one child and know something of the wonder of children. So mused Bob, a young father, to himself. His wife, Donna, was seven months pregnant with their second child, and because of the joy that their oldest child, Elizabeth, had brought them, Bob was keenly anticipating their new bundle of life.

It was amid this joyous expectation that Elizabeth startlingly had caught his attention. For the second time that week at the supper table, while he and Donna were discussing the little one on the way, Elizabeth had complained extensively—something very much unlike her. This time she talked about how her teacher, Mrs. Johnson, had favored a classmate who seemed to get all kinds of special privileges. Elizabeth talked on and on about how she felt slighted because of this unfair treatment. Then she spoke in great detail about a friend in the neighborhood who was moving away. She was going to miss her desperately, she said, and she knew her friend would be very lonely as well after the move.

Bob also saw that Elizabeth had become a little whinier

recently—and she wasn't normally a whiner. It also occurred to him that maybe Elizabeth was reacting to the impending birth of the baby in her own way. Could it be that deep down she wasn't talking solely about her classmate as one who was being favored? Maybe she believed her new sibling on the way was getting more attention. Perhaps Elizabeth also was trying to tell them that, like her neighborhood friend, she had a big change coming in her life which meant she was going to be lonely. Bob had previously been in therapy, and he had learned firsthand that at times when people talk about others they may also be talking about themselves.

Suddenly Bob recalled the story that Elizabeth recently had written for school, a story about a bunny who had been adopted by a family and given a good home. "The bunny was lucky," Elizabeth wrote, "because she had a sister who was still in the pet store and as yet was unadopted." Once again, Bob noted, Elizabeth had been talking about someone who was favored and someone who wasn't—and this time the latter was the poor, lonely bunny who was left behind in the pet store.

The more Bob thought about it, the more logical it seemed that his daughter was dealing with far more about the new baby than he had realized. After all, she had been an only child for seven years, and a very special child at that. And sometimes when you have a special role, you also have the most to lose. Bob decided to listen more closely to Elizabeth to try to confirm his hunch.

A few days later he was home early from work when Elizabeth came home from school. She was fussy from the moment she arrived. Both Bob and his wife tried to comfort their daughter for several minutes. Then Bob decided to make a clear effort to talk about the new baby. Suddenly, Elizabeth erupted in tears, insisting she—Elizabeth—was "no more important than a gnat." Because Bob had heard her previous stories, with their hidden messages, he was able to comfort Elizabeth in a special way and show her that indeed she was still a special child.

Bob had waited until he could have the most effect— when Elizabeth realized her pain—and he took her in his arms and settled her down. Picking up on the emotions she was struggling with, he said to his daughter in her pain, "You know that story of yours about the bunny? Well, if we were in the pet store, we would adopt that little bunny who didn't have a home. We would make sure she would always have a home, just like you do." After being held by her loving father for a few minutes, confirming by deed the loving words of his sensitive story, Elizabeth's mood changed drastically. She immediately began to play and laugh, once again knowing her place in the home was secure.

It would have been very easy for Bob to have simply disciplined Elizabeth for being fussy. But he would have missed out on what deep down really had been bothering her—a fear that the stability of her nurturing environment was under threat.

It would have been very easy for Bob to have simply disciplined Elizabeth for being fussy. But he would have missed out on what deep down really had been bothering her—a fear that the stability of her nurturing environment was under threat. By acknowledging her pain and comforting her, he obtained a far better result than simple (but misdirected) discipline would have.

OUR FIRST GREAT NEED: COMMITMENT

Whether we're a child like Elizabeth or an adult, we see the same concern for "our place" or "our space" wherever we turn. I know of another instance when two young children, whose mother was pregnant, asked their father if one of them would die when the baby came. They reasoned literally, as children often do, that there were only four places at the family table; therefore a new baby meant someone had to give up his or her place. Their parents reassured them they could make more space at the table; but it was only when the baby came that they breathed a sigh of relief, telling their father, "See, we didn't die."

I know of another instance when two young children, whose mother was pregnant, asked their father if one of them would die when the baby came.

When people meet in groups on a regular basis, often they sit in familiar places which eventually become identified with them. After the famed football coach Paul "Bear" Bryant died, an entourage of buses carried mourners from the church service to the grave site some fifty miles away. On the bus carrying a number of former players and coaches, no one sat in the first-row space where Bryant always sat. It was *his* place.

This need to belong and to have a clear-cut space that is ours partly explains our attachment to home and family. It also partly explains why we feel so vulnerable as we move away from familiar environments and why issues such as job security mean more than we realize. The popular hobby of people studying their genealogy is another indication that knowing our place in the scheme of things is one of our most basic needs.

> *And, deep down, we want our nurturing environments to be as absolutely strong as possible because we want to be as strong as we possibly can.*

Yet this need to *belong*, as it is commonly referred to, is much more than that. It is a need to have a place—both literal and emotional—that is *committed to us*. Our environment "builds into us," as do the people in our environment. It is crucial in our development to have a supportive, loving family. And, deep down, we want our nurturing environments to be as absolutely strong as possible because we want to be as strong as we possibly can. I call this the *need for commitment*. The deeper intelligence clearly teaches us that our first and foremost need is the need for *commitment*—and it reinforces to us that it is an ongoing need.

A man named Robert had been in psychotherapy with me for four months when he suggested he was ready to lessen the frequency of his appointments. After he made this request, he continued to speak about other matters—and as usual I sat listening for whatever his deeper intelligence might say about whether this was a good idea.

Soon Robert began talking about how someone had been parking in his assigned space at work. Next, he spent several minutes talking about his son's teacher, who frequently was absent, which had a deleterious effect on his son's performance. Robert also mentioned a friend's son who seemed directionless, moving from one job to another, living with his girlfriend, and unable to make a commitment of marriage to her. Finally, he talked about his wife's job situation where, due to an equipment shortage and poor management, two people were forced to share computer equipment.

It became clear to me through these "revelations" that Robert's deeper intelligence was telling us it wasn't at all a good idea for him to switch to less frequent sessions, because it would undermine the stability he needed. Without question, he had a definite need for his own space and identified with and drew strength from that space. His story about the sneaky parker who used his parking space at work hinted at his desire for a private and predictable "space" with me, his therapist. The story about the often-absent teacher similarly pointed to his need for stability and consistency. And his wife's frustration with having to share her computer with others likewise sounded very much like a desire in Robert to meet with me regularly—alone. In the face of his request to space out his sessions, his deeper intelligence had clearly recommended through "a lack of stability or need of my own space" code to stick to weekly appointments.

Psychotherapy draws much of its power from the fact that a therapist can pledge to a patient a consistent environment that is exclusively theirs. The therapist has the ability to offer the patient an environment that he does not share with anyone else in the world. Every week the therapist reserves the same hour for no one else but the patient, as long as it's necessary. Because of a patient's remarkable capacity to identify with this environment, great potential exists for healing and wholeness. As a therapist keeps a patient's space intact (whole), the patient incorporates that wholeness into his life just as parents can provide a whole or unbroken environment for their developing child.

Psychotherapy draws much of its power from the fact that a therapist can pledge to a patient a consistent environment that is exclusively theirs.

The deeper intelligence is much more aware of our need for a solid framework than is our conscious mind. If this security framework—our need for commitment—is not intact, we will react as Robert did: Although our conscious desire might differ, deep down we will demand to have the commitment we need.

The deeper intelligence is much more aware of our need for a solid framework than is our conscious mind.

We shouldn't be surprised that often we are not aware immediately when there's been a break in our security framework. Our two-level mind is set up to help us initially avoid pain so that when something painful occurs, such as a major disappointment or letdown by a key person, we automatically push it out of our mind. This means we often hide our deepest needs from ourselves, because our needs make us vulnerable. And vulnerability simply is not comfortable.

OUR SECOND GREAT NEED: AUTONOMY

This is one of the most confusing times in my life, Franklin thought to himself as he drove home from his therapist's office. *Even my psychotherapy puzzles me— and I had sought it to bring some clarity to my life.* He wondered if he should change therapists, as his therapy wasn't at all like he'd expected, and certainly not like the movies portrayed it. Nevertheless, he had to admit in the few months he had been in therapy his anxiety attacks were much less frequent.

His mind went back to today's session. He could see Dr. Johnson just sitting there, doing nothing but listening. No chitchat at the beginning of the session, no advice at crucial moments, and even when Franklin had a question Dr. Johnson would usually ask him to keep talking until he could better understand the question. Finally, Franklin thought, *How is this going to help me?*

However, there was this intriguing idea that Dr. Johnson had suggested again today—that Franklin's own mind was trying to guide him to understand some important things about himself. Franklin thought over the session again to see if he couldn't make a bit more sense of it. *Dr. Johnson makes too big a deal of my uncle paying for therapy. After all, he's loaded, and it's nice of him to pay for half of my sessions. These shrinks are expensive, and every little bit helps.*

As Dr. Johnson had asked him to do, Franklin had begun the session talking spontaneously, speaking his mind without screening anything. He remembered telling his doctor, "I've been thinking a lot about my cousin who is coming to visit me. He's coming to town to see a doctor, and not only does he want a place to sleep, but I expect him to hit me up for money before he leaves—his usual strategy. I blame his mother, who was always overinvolved in his life, for not making him grow up. At thirty-two he still lives with her. Because of his helplessness, my cousin twists things so he always feels victimized and can ask others for money. It's like these 'victims' who are always involved in lawsuits and feeling entitled to money. My cousin needs to become more independent."

After that Franklin remembered talking about the baseball game: "Somebody at work gave me some tickets to the game. There was a wreck on the freeway which blocked traffic, and I was late to the game. I didn't think I was going to make it. Anyway, I should have stayed home because we lost the game on account of not having any offense, any power."

He recalled mentioning the article he had read on health care: "I don't think this idea of complete government involvement in health care is a good idea. The government will undercut doctors' fees, and they will lose their motivation. You get what you pay for." Discussing the article had then reminded Franklin of the checks he had forgotten to give Dr. Johnson the week before, one from him and one from his uncle.

Dr. Johnson then made another comment: "You are talking about people who are financially dependent upon others—your cousin; 'victims' who constantly sue others, and people depending on the government for medical care—and how this isn't a good idea. Deep down your mind is trying to tell you that you have a greater need for independence than you realize. Your uncle helping you pay for therapy is unknowingly undermining the independence you are trying to gain."

After that comment Franklin told Dr. Johnson that it would be a real hardship to pay for therapy completely on his own, and that his uncle was quite wealthy and was glad to give him the money. Even so, he told the doctor that he possibly could pay for therapy himself if it was that important.

Later in his session, Franklin mentioned the new stadium that was being built for the baseball team and how terrific it was going to be. Dr. Johnson then pointed out to him that as he was considering paying for therapy himself, his mind went to the idea of a space which carried great opportunity—a way of telling them that he needed his own space completely free of anyone else.

The more he thought about what his therapist was saying, it gradually made some sense. Looking back he could see that he had been too dependent in the past and not taken charge when he should have. He had to admit that he needed to be more assertive, and he hoped that therapy really could help him. Franklin thought to himself, *Maybe Dr. Johnson was right about my uncle helping me pay for therapy not being the best thing for me. But it's so hard to believe I'm telling myself these things I can't feel.* Franklin continued to wonder to himself, *Is my mind really trying to tell me something? Is this my subconscious?*

* * *

Once again we observe an issue come up in therapy— here an outside party paying for therapy—which the patient's deeper intelligence is quite concerned about, and which his conscious mind feels is completely unimportant.

Franklin's experience is not in the least unusual, except that in a way he began to grasp more quickly than most that he truly had another part of him trying to guide him. Many people complete psychotherapy without understanding they possess a deeper intelligence. Even when the message from the deeper intelligence is quite clear, it is never that clear to the conscious mind. This means our conscious minds often overlook or minimize our deepest needs.

Another message from the deeper intelligence is that independence—autonomy—is something we feel passionate about. Independence is directly related to self-worth and self-respect. There is an incredible need within our hearts to express ourselves, in essence to be ourselves. And if someone else does work for us that we should do ourselves, we miss out on an opportunity to realize the potential we know we possess. This eats away at our self-worth. Far more often than we notice it, our deeper intelligence knows it is best for us to handle a task as independently as possible, despite whatever hardship it requires. The deeper intelligence wants us to develop our autonomy.

Side by side with our desire for autonomy, however, lies another part of us that wants to take the easy way, because it requires less effort. Yet this "easy way" in the end robs us of the very character we wish to express. If we are to understand ourselves and reach our potential, we must be aware of the battles we face to declare our independence, many of them subtle—as this story of Slade and his father illustrates.

The father had been burdened by his twenty-year-old son's school performance. The young man, Slade, soon would be entering his junior year in college. *How is he ever going to make it in the business world if he doesn't show more drive?* the father wondered bitterly.

He had stayed on Slade's back at times, perhaps too hard, but this had had no obvious impact. His grades continued to be barely above passing, and he hadn't had any extracurricular involvement except in his fraternity, where most of the young men seemed to be replicas of him.

Slade had made a halfhearted attempt at finding a job that summer, but he insisted that all the good jobs were gone because his college term ran later in the spring than other schools. Briefly the father wondered if he shouldn't have pushed Slade harder to find work. *I remember having to work twelve hours a day when I was his age,* he thought. *And I never had any fun. Life is for living, and I want to give him the things I never had. Maybe later he'll come around.*

He decided as he drove to the golf club for an afternoon golf game with Slade that he would bring up the subject. After the first few holes, after his son had settled into his game, the father asked Slade, "Have you given any thought to your major and your grades?"

In his typical fashion, Slade brushed the comment aside. "Dad, you know golf is a lot more important than school," he joked. "Let's don't mess up a good thing. Let's talk about other things."

Rather than push the issue, the father decided to join in the bantering with his son. Striding side by side up the fairway after their next tee shot, the father mentioned the football team at Slade's school.

Casually, Slade asked his father if he had heard about the coach's son, who was in Slade's class. "He's a real boozer on an ego trip. Everyone knows he's an alcoholic. It's amazing he's been able to stay in school. He never goes to class, and he has just managed to pass by the skin of his teeth. His father must not say much. I don't think the coach is home very often, and he gives his son anything he wants. The father ought to be tougher on the son, the way he is with his players."

For a brief moment, Slade's father thought that, like the coach, maybe he was giving his son too much. But he took comfort that while his son might enjoy a drink or two, Slade wasn't an alcoholic. Then they went on with their golf game.

Was this just a casual conversation between a father and a son with no more meaning than appeared on the surface? Or was there another story here that reflected an attempt on the part of Slade's deeper intelligence to communicate to his father some important changes this dad needed to make in his relationship with his son? If the father had not gotten thrown off track by the details of his son's story and had seen the larger picture, he could have seen how he was behaving in far too many ways like the coach.

In his own way, this father was restricting his son's growth by making him too dependent on him. He couldn't see that buying his son an expensive car, giving him a liberal allowance, letting him do as he pleased with his time without having a summer job, and not setting real standards of accountability for his grades all fostered passivity in his son. If he had been aware of how the deeper intelligence communicates, he could have recognized its messages.

The son, while consciously ignoring his father's confrontation, within a very short period of time had proceeded to tell his dad a story unconsciously designed to point out the mutual blind spots in the father and the son. The father, said the son's deeper mind, was giving the son too much without asking for anything in return—in essence, addicting the son to depending on him. To make sure the father understood the message, the son clearly brought up the subject of grades in his story as if to say, "Here is what causes kids to make bad grades."

What is even more remarkable is that Slade's father fleetingly connected his own parenting to the coach's, but then quickly went into denial. If he had appreciated our great capacity for blind spots and had understood the power of his leadership role as father, he would have been asking himself how he was contributing to his son's problems.

Going one step further, if Slade's father had realized how deep was his son's need for autonomy—for self-respect and achievement—he might have listened for such a key story from the young man.

Somewhere in each person's "heart"— that is, his deeper mind—everyone wants someone to help bring out his best.

If Slade's father had appreciated just how great this need for autonomy and self-expression is, he would have anticipated his son's needs and required more of him. Somewhere in each person's "heart"—that is, his deeper mind—everyone wants someone to help bring out his best.

Another remarkable trait the deeper intelligence possesses is its persistence. If something is wrong, if basic needs are not being met, the deeper intelligence will continue to communicate the problem over and over until it is corrected. Because our deeper mind is so persistent, I am certain Slade's deeper intelligence had made previous attempts to catch his father's attention, as well as his own. Unquestionably, at other crucial moments he would have told similar stories—messages from "down under," which were overlooked.

The two great needs I have mentioned thus far, commitment and autonomy, go together like a hand in a glove; they coexist in an exquisite balance. Living within a strong environment (the first need—commitment) enables us to take the next step of self-expression (the second need—autonomy). Then we are no longer preoccupied with finding security, but instead are free to express ourselves. Finding the grand balance between living within boundaries and having freedom—between commitment and creativity (autonomy at its finest)—is a constant challenge.

OUR THIRD GREAT NEED: INTEGRITY

The deeper intelligence also insists that we have *integrity*. Integrity is total honesty or having the courage to listen consistently to the truth about ourselves, no matter where it leads us.

The words of Dr. Akins's young colleague had stuck in the craw of the experienced psychiatrist. Darrell had told him: "You may think you know something about psychotherapy, but until you've learned to listen to the deeper intelligence you are not going to get all the way home with your patients. I've seen it in my own practice."

Darrell's insinuation bothered Dr. Akins. Not only was Darrell several years younger and less experienced, but he seemed certain that he knew a better way than his elder in the field. Oh, he wasn't really arrogant about his "new approach to therapy"; he was just so blooming enthusiastic—so inflexible—it was irritating.

Dr. Akins always prided himself on being open-minded. That was something that had attracted him to his specialty of psychiatry in the first place—the field's spirit of open-mindedness. Too many times in medical school he had witnessed rigidity among his professors (and classmates), which seemed to stifle constructive curiosity and personal growth.

Ironically, it was because of this very pride he took in being open-minded that Dr. Akins refused to let himself completely dismiss Darrell's comments, even if he had been partially offended. Perhaps at some point he would listen along the lines that Darrell had suggested, just to see what happened—although he was certain he already knew how to listen to his patients.

Shortly after this somewhat intense discussion with Darrell, one of Dr. Akins's patients, Phyllis, called to let him know that the medical workup for her reoccurring abdominal pain had revealed nothing significant. Her physician, Dr. Bryant, was certain Phyllis's symptoms were related to stress, and he had suggested that she use tranquilizers. However, he wanted Dr. Akins to make that decision.

Dr. Akins confirmed to Phyllis that she was indeed "dealing with a lot," mentioned her marital difficulties, and agreed that he would make any necessary decisions about medication for her stress. He said he would call his medical colleague and collaborate with him on her treatment.

At the beginning of Phyllis's next session, Dr. Akins told

her about his brief contact with her physician. Phyllis thanked him for talking with the doctor. "It's good to have two doctors who care about you," she said. Then Phyllis right away began talking about her husband and their difficult marriage. She said, "Once again my husband did something I asked him not to do. He told a friend about how difficult I had said the principal of our son's school is. I didn't want him to tell anyone, because it could get back to the principal. But my husband said he was just trying to help his friend, who was also having problems with the principal."

A few minutes later, when Phyllis mentioned a woman on the P.T.A. board who was always gossiping, it caught Dr. Akins's attention. He thought, *Darrell would find this interesting. She's expressed two thoughts in these first few minutes about people inappropriately talking about others, just after I told her about talking with her family physician.* He reassured himself, however, thinking, *But then, there are a lot of ways to interpret indirect messages. I think she's just beginning to let herself experience her anger in different relationships.*

Only a few minutes later, Dr. Akins noticed that Phyllis spoke with much feeling about a conversation she'd overheard at a cocktail party she'd recently attended. "Some lawyers talk too freely about who their clients are," she said. "I wouldn't like it if they were talking about me publicly. I think they ought to take their clients' privacy more seriously." Dr. Akins noted clearly the third reference to someone having violated confidentiality. But he still wasn't convinced it had anything to do with his having spoken briefly with her physician.

Toward the end of the session, Phyllis made yet another comment which made a partial believer out of Dr. Akins. She described a neighbor by saying, "She's always talking behind her friends' back. No wonder she's on her third marriage."

As much as he didn't want to admit it, Dr. Akins felt

that Phyllis was probably reacting to his discussion with her physician. She was, after all, a very sensitive person—often too sensitive for her own good, he thought. Even so, he decided to say something to let her know he had heard her. He said, "Several times today after I told you about speaking with your family doctor, you have talked about people who betray private communication or talk behind the backs of others. I think perhaps it bothered you more than you know that I spoke with Dr. Bryant."

Phyllis insisted that she had wanted him to speak with her medical doctor and that it didn't bother her in the least. Then she went on immediately to talk about her work with the P.T.A. and her sons' teachers. She noted that one teacher had told her how much better her son was paying attention in class. At the end of the session, Phyllis again thanked Dr. Akins for taking the time to talk with her family doctor.

Dr. Akins had thought it interesting that after he had pointed out all of Phyllis's thoughts about breaks in privacy she had talked about someone (her son) listening better. Perhaps this was an indication, as Darrell might say, that he was "hearing" her well on the so-called deeper level. The therapist shrugged his shoulders. *Maybe this is just another of those gray areas in psychiatry,* he mused. *I still think her main problem is difficulty expressing her anger.*

Ideally, the deeper intelligence, with its phenomenal wisdom, should be able to convince us of its existence. Yet despite some who become convinced of its great power, many like Dr. Akins cannot hear its messages for very long. You see, Dr. Akins reacted self-protectively to the possibility that he had not behaved as ideally as a therapist should. For the most part, he was unwilling to admit he might have done anything outside his awareness, and he was strongly inclined to rationalize his behavior—like we all are. His *externalizing mode* was working overtime, convincing him the patient primarily was talking about someone other than himself. When that occurred, Dr. Akins lacked integrity deep down. In short, he failed to accept responsibility for his actions, failed to own who he was at that moment. When he did, he lacked wholeness.

Yet there is another reason Dr. Akins overlooked the deeper intelligence: *fear of accountability*. There is a part of us that naturally avoids having to be accountable—and the deeper intelligence demands of us a high accountability when it comes to integrity. And to truly hear it, the deeper mind asks a person to submit, in a way, to an authority. The deeper intelligence asks us to give up a great deal personally in order to reap the benefits of its wisdom. We must give up the idea that our conscious minds know the full meaning of integrity.

The breakthrough of deeper intelligence presents to us a second part of ourselves which works in its own way, speaking its own language; it has its own integrity or moral code. This represents a new, higher view of our mind. (The old view of the deeper mind was that it was a vague entity filled mostly with primitive unacceptable wishes classically known as the *id* and an overly harsh conscience called the *superego*.) The new view is that the deeper mind also has a clear perspective of its own, with a marvelously sensitive moral compass that tries to steer us in the ideal direction. Instead of being crude and nondiscriminating, the deeper intelligence is ethically gifted beyond words. Instead of being a monster to be tamed, the deeper mind possesses wisdom to be tapped.

As children we typically have more integrity than when we're older. We haven't yet become as jaded or warped by our world and thus are more authentic and honest. As we "grow up" we study adults to learn how we should behave; we want desperately to find someone who will model integrity. And like all children, we are masters at spotting inconsistencies, plenty of which we find in the adults who populate our lives. In fact we discover too soon that human beings are not just inconsistent, at times they *lie*.

Lying is an assault on reality and therefore on our senses. We are told one thing is reality when, in fact, it is another. Naturally we tend to depend on what we are told, and when we find out reality is the opposite of what we've been told, we cannot escape experiencing chaos, uncertainty, and betrayal. Frustration and anger naturally follow. And now, instead of being in a peaceful state, we are in the midst of the powerful disruptions caused by a lie.

But it isn't just *others* who lie. The breakthrough to the deeper intelligence reveals that not only are we phenomenally astute deep down and possess incredible perceptive abilities, but we also have far greater abilities to lie to ourselves. Often only the deeper intelligence can pick up on blind spots in our integrity. Once we understand what integrity really is, our eyes are opened and we can begin to spot contradictions in ourselves and in others. Then we can understand how we affect others and they affect us.

Once we begin to grasp how limited our conscious minds are in comparison to our deeper intelligence, all sorts of changes can occur in us. We can approach our problems differently. Take therapy, for example: Instead of the therapist acting as the one who possesses all the wisdom, now the patient has the insight and power to guide the therapy. The deeper intelligence of every patient now has the ability to hold the therapist accountable—and does so. In everyday life we can apply the same principles and listen more to others.

The ancient philosopher Diogenes was right. Truth is very difficult to come by, but we must not give up the battle for it just because it's hard. Nevertheless, the myth of the honest man must be given up in order that we might fight the battles we need to fight. If we constantly believe we are people of complete integrity, and that it's those "dishonest people" who have problems telling the truth, we are fooling ourselves. This is the good news / bad news message that the deeper intelligence brings to our self-awareness.

The deeper intelligence—the ultimate realist—reveals both our glory as well as our shame. In the final analysis, this is good news—very good news.

Some may consider this to be a jaded view of humanity. But those who insist on maintaining an idealized view of people (particularly of themselves) will never truly own up to those parts of themselves that cause them and others difficulty. The deeper intelligence—the ultimate realist— reveals both our glory as well as our shame. In the final analysis, this is good news—very good news. Yet only when we look soberly at both our goodness and our failings can we begin to be whole.

Wholeness is at the heart of our need for integrity. In many ways, wholeness is another word for integrity. (Think of the word "integrated.") All three of our great needs—commitment, autonomy, and integrity—point us in one direction, to wholeness. Our *need for commitment* asks for boundaries that are unbroken and thus whole. Our *need for autonomy* asks for a clear identity, to truly let us be our self. And our *need for integrity* asks ourselves and others for consistency and honesty on both levels of our mind.

At the deepest level of our being, we long to be people of wholeness, and we will not rest until this critical goal is achieved.

CHAPTER SIX

Understanding One-to-One Relationships

The need we have throughout our life for important one-to-one relationships cannot be overestimated. We are communal beings; we have not been made to live alone. This is obviously true from the very beginning of life, as two primary one-to-one relationships shape us—one with our mother and one with our father. (Even if one of your parents was absent, you were shaped by that very absence).

Your important one-to-one relationships build into your life uniqueness, affirmation, privacy, self-respect, boundaries, limits, understanding, empathy, and respect. These are all qualities you must possess to get the most out of yourself.

The fact is your life is centered on the quality of your one-to-one relationships—with your spouse, your children, your parents, your friends, your supervisors, and fellow employees at work. Even the slightest disruption or confusion in a key one-to-one relationship can have a major impact, as this story illustrates.

Jonathan, a regional supervisor for his corporation, had not been looking forward to his lunch with Steve, his district sales manager. As Jonathan walked into the picturesque French restaurant in Central Florida, he saw Steve sitting at a table with a slightly forced but not unpleasant smile. Tall, thin, exceedingly polite and soft-spoken—in short, the consummate gentleman—Steve was a man with few enemies. For a moment, Jonathan thought fondly of previous meetings with Steve in this same restaurant. But that only made this meeting more painful, because today Jonathan had to address a major problem with Steve. For some reason Steve's performance had taken a significant nosedive—off some 35 percent. His job was not in danger, because his territory was still performing above average for the company. But Jonathan knew Steve could do better.

It wasn't long into the meeting before Jonathan realized he probably wasn't going to get any real answers from Steve. At different points during their lunch, Jonathan casually brought up the problem, but Steve had nothing to say. Jonathan thought, *Either he has minimized his district's performance as part of the usual ups and downs of doing business, or he seems genuinely puzzled. It's always one of these two responses.*

Then toward the end of the meal, Steve mentioned in passing the problems his wife was having in recovering from her hysterectomy and how the recovery had taken longer than he had anticipated. Jonathan began to listen a little more acutely. Recently he had begun to learn about the deeper intelligence. *Perhaps Steve has been more upset over his wife's surgery than he realizes,* he thought.

A few minutes later Steve caught Jonathan's attention again when he casually mentioned that his father recently had stopped through town while on a vacation. Steve added, "He's been in bad health. He was never there when I was growing up—my folks divorced when I was three." Jonathan began to wonder to himself if Steve wasn't reacting to the stress of his wife and his father having had health problems.

Suddenly it occurred to Jonathan that he had had much less contact with Steve in the last year. Perhaps Steve has been reacting to that, too. *He's done so well in the past, I'd sort of forgotten about him,* Jonathan mused. As if Steve were reading Jonathan's mind, he casually concluded, "I've really missed our lunches here. We need to do this more often, like we used to."

Jonathan was now certain Steve was reacting to a number of stresses involving separation and fear of separation. His wife, his father, and even his boss were all either distant or potentially so. He decided not to confront Steve; instead, he resolved to meet more often with him. But it is clear that Steve had an inordinate number of disruptions in his primary one-to-one relationships. As is so often the case, his performance reflected these stresses, speaking volumes about the importance of close relationships in our adult lives, no matter who we are.

Another story, based on a therapy encounter, also illustrates how our deeper intelligence insists that all of us need key one-to-one, committed relationships.

From the moment she entered the consultation room, Gwen made plain to Dr. Roberts, her new psychiatrist, that she knew what she wanted in therapy, only contradictorily, she was setting up a situation where her deepest needs for commitment would be violated. Unknowingly, she was violating her deepest needs for stability.

As she told him, "Several years ago I was in therapy when I became depressed right after my second child was born. I saw a psychiatrist for about six months and haven't had any real problems since. For the last six months I have been battling depression again, and I thought that I ought to see someone. That's when Dr. Leitman gave me your name.

"I think I just need a few appointments to talk things out, nothing prolonged. Maybe if I could see you a couple of times a month to start with it would help—whenever you can work me into your schedule. I have thought a good deal about my problems and know myself pretty well. I was a psychology major. There may be some things from my past I might want to explore, and I wonder if you do hypnosis? You might want to talk to my previous psychiatrist."

In his usual fashion, Dr. Roberts had remained quiet from the beginning of therapy letting Gwen do the talking in order to hear what she communicated. Now, fifteen minutes into the session, far different thoughts about Gwen were occurring to him than to her. Privately, he thought, *She thinks she knows what she wants, but it won't be long before unknowingly she tells me a far different story about what her real needs are. I have never seen it fail yet. She thinks she wants an irregular environment here with an occasional session, but that would mean deep down that I would fail to make as strong a commitment as she needs. I predict that soon she will talk about other relationships where people break commitments and shouldn't.*

His expectations came to pass rather quickly. Soon Gwen casually mentioned, "The one thing that bothers me is my ex-husband. He rarely sees our daughter, and I think it has a very negative effect on her. I know what it feels like. My parents divorced when I was eight years old. My father was never around much, either before or after the divorce.

"My present husband hasn't been much help as a stepfather. He is not a drinker like my first husband, George, was, and he is a nice guy and all; but he is always gone hunting and fishing. I think he loves the outdoors more than he loves people."

Once again Gwen had triggered a series of thoughts in Dr. Roberts's mind: *There it is. She's talking about how a number of people aren't living up to commitments and are never there. She is not just talking about her daughter's needs, but also about her own.*

Dr. Roberts thought about other patients who had made proposals that he knew would spell trouble for them, who unknowingly would ask him to break a commitment to them at the very same moment they would be telling him how important it was that he keep his commitment to them. Even though Gwen's conscious mind presented the idea of an occasional hit-and-miss appointment schedule, her deeper intelligence knew that she needed a committed slot. Again, confidently Dr. Roberts knew that if Gwen would keep talking, she would eventually tell him why she was setting up a situation which violated her deepest needs.

Certainly, we would need to hear the rest of this and other sessions to completely verify that Dr. Roberts's hunches and interpretations were accurate. But Gwen's words are very instructive. In order that Dr. Roberts wouldn't miss the message, immediately after she requested irregular appointments, her deeper intelligence started presenting stories about the price of broken commitments in relationships: Her father not being there for her, her new husband being absent, and so on. The deeper intelligence is very convincing when we see a clear trigger (the request for an irregular appointment) followed first by stories (of broken relationships) which perfectly fit descriptions of irregular environments, and then by stories which suggested ways to have more committed relationships.

In Gwen's case, the left brain was saying, "I want a very loosely defined therapy with irregular appointments and hypnosis where patient and doctor's boundaries are blurred as they merge with each other." Her right brain was completely rejecting this idea by repeatedly saying that what she needed was a solid, stable, well-defined one-to-one relationship. Gwen's stories were acting as a corrective to show Dr. Roberts that deep down her proposal for irregular therapy was not a good idea and that Gwen's conscious mind had a defect and a blind spot.

Here we clearly see the punishing intelligence in action, as Gwen had come to the self-defeating decision that what she needed was a lack of stability when in fact she needed more. Although the punishing intelligence is outside of conscious awareness, nevertheless since it often has primary control over our conscious feelings, for the sake of simplicity, I will on occasion refer to the punishing intelligence as a part of the left brain.

THE NEED FOR THE ONE-TO-ONE

The breakthrough to the deeper intelligence underscores what we have known all along—that the fundamental bedrock of our lives is the one-to-one relationship. Of course, this starts with our parents, then later in adult life, most individuals enter a permanent one-to-one—marriage—which holds out the promise of stability throughout life.

The deeper intelligence reveals to us that our primary one-to-one relationships in life are far more important than we have ever realized, no matter how much we have appreciated them consciously. From the very first minute a patient enters psychotherapy, she is fundamentally concerned that the one-to-one relationship with a therapist be as strong and committed as possible (as Gwen just demonstrated).

The deeper intelligence reveals to us that our primary one-to-one relationships in life are far more important than we have ever realized, no matter how much we have appreciated them consciously.

108

Consistently, a patient's right-brain needs for stability and strength in the therapeutic relationship are clearly greater than the more superficial left-brain needs. The same need for commitment is there in all of us in our primary relationships outside of therapy as well. (If we think about it, our three greatest needs are only defined within the context of a one-to-one relationship.)

Diagram A shows how we can view all our important relationships as intimate one-to-ones, with mutual respect for the individuality of the other within a stable environment.

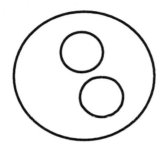

Diagram A

THE SIGNIFICANT BOUNDARIES OF THE ONE-TO-ONE

The deeper intelligence also teaches us something else about our one-to-one relationships—that they can be disrupted far more easily than we have ever previously understood. It is critical that we broaden our understanding of where the boundaries of our one-to-one relationships really are.

Are we who we think we are? Do we really know the boundaries of our awareness and exactly when and how we are influenced by others? And do we know exactly how we influence others? Do we vastly underestimate our complete identity, and in so doing underestimate our

109

marvelous hidden skills of perception and analysis? Is it possible we each possess far keener and deeper intuition than we ever imagined?

One way to answer these questions is by examining boundaries, which we must maintain to truly be ourselves and to be whole. Clear, firm boundaries declare who we are. Boundaries of stability, identity, and independence help us distinguish ourselves from others. Our boundaries make us ourselves and no one else.

Yet our boundaries of stability and autonomy are much more fragile than we realize. We can easily be hurt by others when they destroy important personal boundaries of ours (often without our knowing it). A very simple but common story reveals this truth.

In the still of the early morning summer air, Katherine relaxed after a challenging, self-imposed workout on her Stair-Master and treadmill. Her mind was exceedingly clear. Working out often had this effect on her.

As she began to gather her suitcases to begin packing for her trip in two days—her annual ten-day visit with her parents—she suddenly realized perhaps why she and her husband, Victor, had been fighting for the last few days. *I'll bet it's the fact that I'm leaving for ten days that upsets him,* she told herself. The more she thought about it, she was amazed she hadn't recognized the pattern before. Every time during their four years of marriage that she'd gone by herself to visit her parents in the summertime, Victor had gotten upset.

What was it he said last night while he was reading the magazine? she tried to recall. She remembered he had casually mentioned a story about a home for abandoned children. Several neighbors were protesting that the home was being planned in their neighborhood. Victor had seemed particularly angry at those people for being so insensitive.

Katherine recognized that *abandonment* had been on Victor's mind. She saw, too, that for some reason during these infrequent periods of arguing, she wasn't as able to deflect his irritability or to control hers.

Katherine thought back to a few nights before when Victor had watched a television show he didn't normally watch. It had to do with a man who didn't want his girlfriend to take a job in another town. At the end of the show, when the girlfriend had changed her mind, Victor casually commented, "Hollywood always has these romantic endings. In real life she would have moved to another town."

One thought led to another and Katherine remembered something else. While driving together to work a few days before, seemingly out of the blue, her husband asked what she thought about a local man who had killed himself after he'd lost his business and his wife had divorced him. At the time Katherine hadn't made much of it. But now she wondered if Victor was thinking a lot about abandonment because that's what he felt deep down but couldn't admit. Maybe it was too painful to allow himself to admit it. It certainly seemed to fit. Victor was from an especially close family and tended to establish close relationships. *He is basically a good husband*, Katherine thought, *other than during these particularly difficult moments.* Katherine was sure now that the original thought which had popped into her head had been verified. She wasn't sure what to do with the information, but she was mildly upset with herself for not seeing the obvious before. *Perhaps,* she pondered, *I can help cut down on the anger that seems to flare up between us whenever I'm going away.*

If Katherine had been as aware of herself as she was of her husband, Victor, she would have noticed that several times during the past week she had made passing comments about separation. She also had been particularly occupied with a friend's sister who was dying with cancer. She had realized that, strangely enough, she wasn't actually that close to this friend.

Victor himself had not at all been aware of any particular pattern to his arguments with his wife. Nor was he conscious of any particular feelings of abandonment in relation to his wife's going away. His initial reaction, when Katherine gently told him what she thought was going on, was one of genuine surprise—and then mostly denial. Victor didn't know how to listen to his deeper intelligence; but his wife did.

Clearly, Victor's personal boundary sensitivities were much greater than he realized. A hidden part of him was in pain and strongly reacted to his wife's going away. But his left brain was telling him that Katherine's going away was no big deal. Of course, he was aware he would miss her, and he was willing to consider that perhaps he had been more irritable; but that was about the extent of his understanding.

When the boundaries of our personality are being affected outside of our awareness, often we react with anger or in other unhealthy ways, which usually only make the problem worse.

On the other hand, Victor's right brain was telling him he was aware that Katherine's going away was greatly affecting him. He was feeling as if he were a child in an orphanage who experienced the abandonment of a parent; or a man whose girlfriend was moving away and would never come back; or a man who had just lost everything, including his wife, and was feeling suicidal. Deep inside Victor was distraught and wanted to escape the pain. Is it any wonder he wanted to hide these feelings from himself? Who wants to face that kind of pain if he doesn't have to?

Victor's denial of his problem caused his wife a lot of distress and also contributed to his own misery. This is a good example of why we must understand where our boundaries are. When the boundaries of our personality are being affected outside of our awareness, often we react with anger or in other unhealthy ways, which usually only make the problem worse. In a real way, we become our own victims.

In this situation we recognize that we are far more powerful people than we realize, with a striking hidden capacity to influence others. Just how powerfully and how frequently we use our influence, only the deeper intelligence can tell us, because often we are unaware where our boundaries start and end. Yet we must appreciate where our boundaries are to see who we truly are and how we affect others. We must also appreciate (as we saw Susan and Gwen do) that surprisingly we can set ourselves up for boundary violation. Why we do this takes us to the core of who we are.

The strength of the environment, the commitment each person in a one-to-one makes to the other, and the ongoing respect of each other's individuality within the relationship offers incredible strength. *Yet it also brings about an incredible amount of fear.* The closer we are to someone—the more we invest in him, the more we love him—the more potential that person has to hurt us. Generally speaking, people vastly underestimate just how great this hurt can be. The fear of being hurt exerts a much more powerful influence at the core of our closest relationships than we think.

On the one hand, there is the fear we could lose the relationship once it is established. Someone can reject us in two ways: They can leave us overtly by walking away, or covertly by emotionally abandoning us. But there is potentially an even greater loss. If we are truly attached to someone, we can lose them permanently: He or she can die. In permanent relationships, such as our family of origin or marriage, the death of a loved one is guaranteed. And the closer we are to those loved ones, the more this separation hurts.

In the back of our minds, the very moment we enter a committed relationship, we are clearly aware that at some point we are going to be hurt. Furthermore, as we face reality, another powerful truth confronts us: our own eventual death. So, close relationships mean security, but they equally mean terrible, dreaded pain. We have this terribly mixed connection of life and death to close relationships. This means on one level we link closeness with death. So it is not hard to see how we can also dread the very type of relationship we desire, because of the constant death anxiety it prompts in our mind.

But there is more. Not only do we associate abandonment and death with closeness; we also fear what can happen if someone *stays around*. The closer we are to others, the more we see what they are really like—and the more they see who *we* really are. Even the best of us are far from perfect. We all, deep down, have powerful and mixed motives. There's not a one of us who isn't competitive and selfish, who isn't above retaliating or holding a grudge. This can be a frightening prospect. Ridicule or other forms of abuse are possibilities. Indeed, anyone we get close to invariably will hurt us at some point. And the closer we become, the more deeply we will hurt.

Already we can begin to understand that the pressures to avoid true intimacy are great. Since one-to-ones unquestionably bring out our deepest flaws, we have a powerful tendency to settle for "compromised" relationships—those in which others don't truly get to know us. That way we don't have to face ourselves either, because we hate seeing our flaws.

Thus, the pressure to escape a one-to-one relationship can be as great as the forces that attracted us so strongly in the first place.

The price tag for true intimacy goes higher and higher. Thus, the pressure to escape a one-to-one relationship can be as great as the forces that attracted us so strongly in the first place. To comprehend our fears in this area, we must appreciate how often we attempt to escape one-to-ones—the very relationships we desperately need.) There are three ways we obliterate or modify our private, one-to-one relationships. The most obvious way of escape is simply to leave the relationship, to walk away. (See Diagram B.)

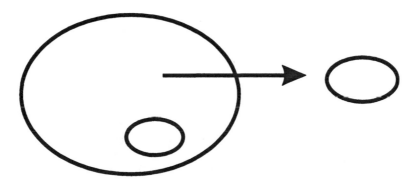

Diagram B

Second, we can change a one-to-one by bringing in a third party (or a fourth party; groups also count) to act as a buffer. Then immediately we have changed a frightening one-to-one into a group. (See Diagram C.)

115

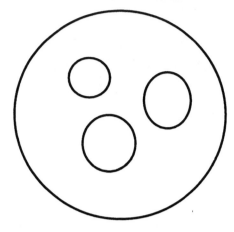

Diagram C

Third, and this is the most subtle avoidance of all, as well as the most common—we can lose ourselves in another person. We merge with someone else and give up our own identity. (See Diagram D.)

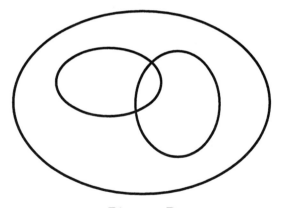

Diagram D

There are many different ways we can merge in an unhealthy fashion, but the most common ones are not speaking up when we should, letting someone else speak for us. There is a point in any relationship where not speaking up violates ourself and the other person.

*This is the most subtle avoidance of
all, as well as the most common—we
can lose ourselves in another person.*

SECURITY ANXIETY

Because of the strong one-to-one relationships we've
had in the past, we recognize when we find a supportive
one-to-one relationship, and immediately we draw
strength from it. The deeper intelligence knows we should
seek this out for our own good. For example, from the
moment he enters the room, a patient coming to psychotherapy instinctively begins reading the therapist and his
environment for signs of stability. When the therapist
maintains a high level of security, the deeper intelligence
appreciates it beyond belief and responds with improved
functioning.

Strangely enough, however, whenever the patient experiences the security he needs, he reacts on another level
with extreme fear. In other words, the very security he
demands also causes him great fear—what is referred to
as "security anxiety." Many times security anxiety stems
from frightening experiences we have had in close relationships, because what once was a stable relationship
now has been linked with pain. As we will see, this
security anxiety is what causes the punishing intelligence
to overreact.

The punishing intelligence is quite perceptive and
brings out our greatest fear. (The problem is that it
magnifies the fear to the extreme conclusion that we will
always be hurt in close relationships or situations.) Psychotherapy is designed to bring this awareness captive,
and through the light of the deeper intelligence to bring

the punishing intelligence—and the misguided behavior that is urged—under control.

> *Strangely enough, however, whenever the patient experiences the security he needs, he reacts on another level with extreme fear. In other words, the very security he demands also causes him great fear—what is referred to as "security anxiety."*

Indeed, what the deeper intelligence teaches unmistakably is exactly what Jesus said two thousand years ago—that knowing the truth is what sets us free. If we can face the fears that control us, we can eventually overcome them. There is something remarkably freeing about facing who we are.

> *I can say without qualification that security anxiety is universal and is a primary driving force in everyone's life.*

I can say without qualification that *security anxiety is universal and is a primary driving force in everyone's life.* Part of this is because many people—many more than we have recognized—have had frightening experiences in enclosed situations which have shaped their lives. Because of our perceptiveness and built-in ability to respond to familiar triggers, we are much more vulnerable to being reminded than we realize.

We only need to look around us to see subtle manifestations of security anxiety, many of which have devastating effects. Divorces, extramarital affairs, abandoned children, alienation between parents and children, or alienation between once-good friends can be manifestations of this most deep-seated of anxieties. Also, disturbing traits such as an inability to make commitments, an inability to complete tasks, chronic lateness to appointments, making frequent and unproductive job changes, making unnecessary and disturbing moves, functioning poorly at work, having a pattern of troubled marriages—all are signs of someone who is afraid of living or staying in definite situations. This fear is far more prevalent than we might think.

INTIMACY: OUR GREATEST NEED, OUR GREATEST FEAR

A story from a research project in a department of psychology, which involved studying how people behave in elevators, gives us a unique picture of how we all view committed (enclosed) relationships in part of our deeper mind.

We've all learned the proper social etiquette of elevators: Don't establish eye contact, don't converse, look straight ahead, don't touch anyone.

Elevator behavior is so fascinating that a few years ago a psychology department sponsored a research project in which volunteers got onto elevators and intentionally broke the "rules." The volunteers stared at others and at times attempted to talk with them. To the project director's surprise, the volunteers kept quitting. They found it

119

so extremely uncomfortable to stare at others on elevators they could not complete the project!

Such a response was to be expected, because for all of us, elevator anxiety is just another indicator of what we paradoxically both deeply long for and fear: intimacy.

The deeper intelligence does us a superb favor: It identifies the major dilemma in the life of every person—we long to be close to others while at the same time being deeply afraid of such close encounters. This is the puzzling, maddening paradox of intimacy. These opposing currents of emotion at the core of our being explain why we behave in perplexing ways, as the following story reveals.

Bradley was enjoying the "feel" of his new car as he drove up to the red-brick educational building to let his two young children off for Sunday school. Arriving at the rear entrance, Bradley and his wife, Sheila, got out of the car to open the doors for their two daughters. At that moment, one of their good friends, Ann, was walking out the door of the building. Thinking Sheila was going to get back into the car with Bradley, Ann admired the new car and asked for a ride in it to the church two blocks away. Bradley held open the passenger door for her and said brightly, "Jump in. Sheila's staying with the kids to help their teacher."

Ann was pleasant enough on the two-block ride to the church, making small talk about the new car. But Bradley quickly sensed she was very uncomfortable. This was verified by another friend, Frank, who saw them drive up to the church.

Frank told Bradley later, "When you stopped, Ann shot out of that car as if she were in a cannon." Bradley laughed off Ann's discomfort. She was the wife of one of the deacons, and perhaps she wanted to avoid anything that might make others wonder why she was alone with a man other than her husband. After all, she was in a responsible role and probably wanted to avoid any hint of scandal.

Twenty minutes later, during a Sunday school class she taught for junior high girls, Ann for some reason changed the emphasis of her lesson. Bradley casually overheard her saying to another mother after the class, "We talked a lot about Daniel in the lions' den, more than I had planned on." For some reason outside of her immediate awareness, Ann had spent more time than planned on the story of a person trapped in a cage of lions.

Is it possible that Ann's short ride in the car had anything to do with what she talked about in the next thirty minutes? Or am I overinterpreting here?

When we begin to appreciate just how sensitive we are to enclosed, one-to-one relationships, Ann's reaction does not seem so strange at all.

Even the possibility we could fear stability is striking, but this unquestionably is one of the central insights the deeper intelligence has revealed. This unrecognized fear has a lot to do with why all of us are prone to making bad choices.

CHAPTER SEVEN

Why We Make Bad Choices

The gentle chirping of the crickets and bleating of the katydids in the encircling woods accompanied occasional rushes of a cool spring breeze—another symphony from nature in the remaining twilight of the day. The sounds surrounded the two friends sitting on the porch of the mountain cottage. But Bart's internal state did not reflect the magnificent peace of the outdoors that surrounded him as he listened to his friend Douglas. All was well with nature, but all was not well with Bart because of what his friend was telling him. Douglas had asked Bart to take a ride with him to his cabin, a short drive from town.

As Bart sat patiently listening to Douglas, he became more and more uneasy. Douglas was seriously contemplating leaving his wife, Jennifer. Douglas confided, "I know this will hurt the kids, but I really think I am in love with Sandra. It happened so fast. Maybe she reminds me of Becky."

Becky had been Douglas's old girlfriend in high school who, as Douglas said, "I don't think I ever got over. Remember when I had that freak infection when I was in high school, and I ended up having surgery and being bedridden for three months? Becky visited me every day.

I might have married her if she had been able to stay true and blue, but she always had that wandering eye. I think that's what being from a broken family did to her. When she broke up with me to date my best friend, she had no idea how she hurt me."

Bart had been saying very little, nodding only occasionally, as Douglas clearly needed to talk. Maybe that is why he was listening more intently than usual—that, and the seriousness of the topic. Suddenly a thought almost bowled him over: *Wasn't Douglas describing himself to a "T" when he talked about his old girlfriend? Someone who had a wandering eye and who was hurting another person with unfaithful, wavering behavior? Was Douglas confessing without knowing it?*

In the meantime, Douglas had shifted his monologue to another topic, this time complaining about his relationship with his company president. Douglas said the president was habitually running around on his wife with a number of different women. Douglas's support for his boss was dwindling daily, not just because of his indiscretions, he said, but because his boss also wasn't much of a leader. He saw the president as indecisive—making commitments and them backing out—and as a result, he was gradually self-destructing, probably taking the company with him because he was so careless.

Bart was dumbstruck. Again Douglas spoke of someone who was doing almost exactly what Douglas himself was doing. A number of questions raced through Bart's mind: *Should I tell him he's really talking about himself? Is it my place to tell him what I think?* The more Bart contemplated this, the more he thought Douglas was indeed confessing. Bart knew a lot of marriages worse than Douglas's, and he had seen more than one person make the mistake of leaving his or her spouse for what seemed like greener pastures.

Exactly what Bart should have said and when are different issues. But unquestionably Douglas appeared to have a clear, though perhaps hidden, awareness that the meaning of his planned actions were far different from what he thought they were. If Bart had understood even better how the mind worked, he would have picked up on a very important clue in Douglas's communication. Not only was Douglas implying he was behaving like his old girlfriend and his boss; he also dropped a major clue as to why. *Deep down he was feeling trapped and endangered, like the time he was ill and had surgery as a teenager.* Also, he knew in the back of his mind that, just as his girlfriend Becky had left him to date his best friend, he was contemplating reenacting the same trauma with his wife by considering leaving her.

For some reason Douglas was experiencing his marriage as a dangerous trap and thought he had to get out (almost certainly because he had unfinished business from traumas in close relationships). He was on the verge of making a life-changing decision based on the limited knowledge of his conscious feelings (which told only 10 percent of the whole story).

This happens millions of times a day, to millions of people, often with devastating results. These bad decisions are driven by fear—fear of a one-to-one relationship or the equivalent. If Douglas had appreciated how misleading his conscious feelings could be, he might have been open to looking at himself in a deeper and more accurate way. But this had occurred with him because of two remarkable qualities of the human mind: First, the mind scans every environment for comparisons to previous environments. And second, it automatically and unconsciously links present environments to previous ones.

Because we all possess a deep-seated fear of one-to-one relationships, particularly heightened if we have had significant traumatic experiences in enclosed situations, this fear comes into play in our lives much more often than we realize. *Bad choices* are, in the final analysis, many times prompted by this fear.

The fear of being enclosed or entrapped too often rules our lives, unless we recognize it for the distortion of reality that it is. Fear of intimacy, or "security anxiety," is a primary, driving force daily in the lives of all human beings. Let me give you an example from psychotherapy.

ANATOMY OF A POOR DECISION

Psychiatrist Ed Pinkerton was devoted to his patients, going to extra lengths and even hardships to make sure they had the kind of environment they needed. He listened closely to every word out of their mouths and was attentive to their every action. His single goal was to help them understand themselves.

Virtually 100 percent of sexually-abused patients who are seriously confronting this past trauma, like Deborah, eventually become uncomfortable in therapy and want to leave.

Even so, Dr. Pinkerton wasn't surprised when his patient Deborah had said she was going to change doctors. Virtually 100 percent of sexually-abused patients who are seriously confronting this past trauma, like Deborah, eventually become uncomfortable in therapy and want to leave, especially if they are attempting to face their pain through the perceptive eyes of the deeper intelligence.

The way she put it that day, "You just aren't giving me enough feedback or guiding me enough. I think I need a different kind of therapy. You sometimes seem cold and uninvolved, though I think you're a nice man who means well."

He had heard it countless times before—the patient's superficial intelligence speaking in order to hide from the deeper intelligence. He knew that if Deborah would continue talking, she would give him more than enough information about why she was running from what she needed. Given enough time, her right brain would completely contradict what her left brain seemed so certain of.

Shortly after her announcement, Deborah told the therapist that her mother was worried about Deborah's father becoming an alcoholic. Dr. Pinkerton thought, *Already she recognizes that for me to begin a question-and-answer approach would be like an addiction. She is trying to depend on me for some reason, and she knows it's wrong. Now she's going to tell me why she wants to relate to me in this unhealthy way. Instead of depending upon herself and her deeper intelligence to guide her, asking me to lead her is like an alcoholic who can't solve his problem without depending on something besides himself.*

Deborah then mentioned her daughter Ann: "She wanted to change teachers, because her teacher—who is excellent—demands a lot. But I wouldn't let her. She can learn a lot from that teacher. Yet Ann is overly sensitive to any correction from me, which causes her to get down on herself. Her brother is somewhat like that, but he recently learned the value of sticking out a difficult situation. He learned that healthy criticism wouldn't kill him. Earlier in the year he wanted to quit football, but my husband wouldn't let him. Eventually, he came to love it and actually excelled at it."

Dr. Pinkerton took notice of the two references to sticking out a difficult situation. Deborah then casually mentioned that for some reason she was less depressed. She also noted, "My husband has been a better listener lately."

Deborah continued by complaining briefly about her in-laws and mentioned her neighbor who had been through hard times. "Four years ago she had a severe boating accident. Another boat hit hers around twilight. They didn't see each other. She ended up having surgery for a fractured leg and nearly died on the operating table because of some type of allergic reaction."

By patiently waiting, Dr. Pinkerton had gained the information he needed. The deeper intelligence virtually never lets a person down at a crucial moment and this was one of them. Any time a patient tries to pull out of the protected learning environment she needs—a hard but necessary school—her deeper mind tries to tell her to stick it out. This is a sterling example of how the deeper intelligence attempts to overcome the punishing intelligence, which is again overreacting and urging bad choices.

These stories—the daughter who needed to stay with a challenging teacher, the son who learned the value of not quitting because something was difficult, and the husband who was becoming a good listener—were the deeper intelligence's warnings to Deborah about the falseness of her drive to switch doctors (and the recognition as well that Dr. Pinkerton was a very good listener).

Dr. Pinkerton put these stories together. But still he wanted Deborah to mention her sexual abuse, so he could tie it all together for her. *Yet was there still time left in the session?*

As if Deborah's deeper intelligence were reading his mind, a few minutes later she talked about the fact that her church was going to have a workshop for victims of sexual abuse. She wasn't sure if she would open up and share anything about her personal life, but she was determined to go to the meeting. Now Deborah had given a clear—albeit indirect—tie-in between all her previous stories and her having been sexually abused. She was spelling out why she really wanted a different therapy. Deborah's left brain was telling her that she needed a better therapist, but her right brain, her deeper intelligence, was telling her that she was in precisely the right therapy and should stick it out.

Her thoughts of two boats colliding, a fractured leg, and surgery revealed that this was the devastating way she experienced the sexual abuse as a child. No wonder she didn't want to bring it up and face it; but her right brain actually was doing her a favor, pushing her like a demanding teacher to get the best out of herself. Her deeper intelligence was saying to her, "See, this is what you have to face to be free."

At that point, Dr. Pinkerton pointed out to Deborah that her relationship with him was triggering her unrecognized fear of one-to-ones, which she saw as tremendously dangerous because of her early experience of being sexually abused. Eventually Deborah saw the connection.

Why, you may ask, would Deborah want to leave an environment like the one Dr. Pinkerton provided, which was so nurturing and potentially freeing? Why was she on the verge of making a bad decision?

The punishing intelligence attempts to negate the healthy messages from the deeper intelligence. The punishing intelligence wants us to suffer.

Making bad decisions was a pattern in Deborah's life, particularly with her tendency to abuse alcohol and prescription drugs. And if we look back at the session just described, we will see that Deborah answered these questions. Her bad choices stemmed from two sources. One was fear. Because of her early perverted experience, in which she experienced an attack instead of a stabilizing influence in her life (a strong one-to-one with an adult), she learned to fear close relationships. She came to associate the very stability she needed with horrible trauma. And because of her mind's self-protective mechanism, she over-read all one-to-ones as being as dangerous as the one-to-one in which she was repeatedly hurt as a child.

The second reason Deborah made bad choices was guilt. Like her daughter, who tended to condemn herself, Deborah condemned herself. Typically, when something went wrong, deep down she blamed herself. A part of her then wanted to suffer—so she sought out disturbing compromised relationships or behaviors that secretly punished her. Here her punishing intelligence showed its face again. The punishing intelligence attempts to negate the healthy messages from the deeper intelligence. The punishing intelligence wants us to suffer.

Knowing that the punishing intelligence exists and comprehending our fear of a one-to-one, we are in a position to better understand ourselves. Thus we can understand people like Douglas or like Deborah, who at crucial moments are prone to make a bad choice and to move away from the very security they desperately need. Then we can understand why people foolishly destroy one-to-ones—by never making a commitment, by infidelities, or by leaving a marriage deep down they don't truly want to leave.

REENACTMENT: REPEATING THE MISTAKES OF THE PAST

Many people, after the fact, realize how mistaken were their decisions. Recently a lady wrote Ann Landers to prevent someone else from giving up on a marriage, as the reader had. She had encouraged her husband's involvement with a recently-divorced female friend by suggesting he help with the woman's household chores.

When her husband "fell in love" with the friend and asked for a divorce, the lady gave it to him without a contest. Three months later the husband realized his error, asked his wife for a second chance, and she refused, thus propelling her husband into a marriage with her former friend.

A few months later, terribly lonely and witnessing her kid's devastation as a result of the divorce, she realized the three bad choices she had made—enabling her husband to develop a relationship with the friend, failing to fight for her husband and marriage, and finally refusing a reconciliation.[1] Each choice created distance in the one-to-one relationship.

If this lady had been able to access her deeper intelligence beforehand, I am certain she would have made better decisions.

The deeper intelligence has done us a favor. It has helped us to see the battle we all must fight in our close relationships and how great the pressure is on us to distance ourselves in various ways from the intimate relationships we really want.

When we distance ourselves from others, we often are reenacting patterns in relationships we learned from others. In reenactments, we assume familiar roles for ourselves and, thus, for others.

Many times a person's reenactment occurs only after a long number of years, because he has hidden his pain so well that he finally reaches a point where he can no longer contain it. Then sudden, "uncharacteristic" changes in his behavior at crucial moments reveal the reenactment.

For example, a delayed reenactment might be an extramarital affair in middle age by a previously loyal spouse, or sudden abandonment by a normally loyal person (as Douglas wanted to abandon his wife). Or an alcoholic who slips and resumes drinking—disappointing his wife and children—may be reenacting the hurt he experienced at the hands of his alcoholic father. A woman who has a history of repeated, guilt-ridden, extramarital affairs may be inflicting the same damage on herself and her spouse as was inflicted on her as a child by a parent who betrayed her. A person who, despite feeling guilty, repeatedly breaks promises can be reenacting how he was disappointed by important others at crucial moments in his life. All of these reenactments have one feature in common—a person violates his own needs and the needs of others in a false attempt to find relief from emotional pain.

When we understand the tendency people have to move away from enclosed one-to-ones, we then can understand why they move away from good situations that in many ways remind them of a former, negative enclosed one-to-one.

Even positive enclosed situations—those with definite boundaries in which we experience our individuality—can easily take on the meaning of entrapping, enclosed situations to us on the second level of our mind. Steady jobs, steady relationships, stable homes, and a place in the community are environments that at times can cause us to react very strongly. We can feel closed in and threatened in these environments, just as we do in close relationships. The more definite the environment, the stronger the potential for a strong, hidden reaction to it. Even the people who seemingly settle into marriages, job, and their community can subtly settle for compromises in their degree of commitment and fail to get the most out of their lives.

THE DILEMMA

In short, we all are in a bind to one degree or another. The very stability (love) we deeply desire in a primary one-to-one relationship, we also fear. How much we distance ourselves from the healthy one-to-one relationships we need depends in part upon how much we have been hurt in previous close relationships. Those who have been hurt the most tend to make the worst choices in one-to-ones later, because they have the most to overcome to establish trust. However, we each have a significant amount of stability anxiety no matter how seemingly healthy our background. Rarely do we recognize this anxiety (or the pressure to distance ourselves from a one-to-one), which means we must look for its manifestations.

If we know the three principles by which we all function and thrive—commitment, autonomy, and integrity—we can then honestly examine each relationship we find ourselves in.

Given our universal human tendency to often bury our most important motivations, how can we begin to know ourselves better? While each of us will answer that question in our own way over the course of our lives, there are some guiding principles we can live by. First, if we know the three principles by which we all function and thrive— commitment, autonomy, and integrity—we can then honestly examine each relationship we find ourselves in.

For example, Douglas, who wanted to leave his wife, and Deborah, who wanted to leave her therapist, could have asked themselves if in their decisions they were violating any of these three laws. In Douglas's case, we see that he was violating the principles of commitment and integrity. In Deborah's case, she could have spotted one of several contradictions. For example, Dr. Pinkerton was offering her autonomy, yet she wanted him to violate this need in her by guiding her (telling her what to think about) instead of Deborah taking responsibility and assertively allowing her deeper intelligence to express itself. If she had known these fundamental rules of relationships in life, she would have known that Dr. Pinkerton was masterfully meeting those needs and could have responded accordingly.

If both Douglas and Deborah had had an understanding of how afraid we all are of one-to-one relationships, they would have been more attuned to their real needs. And if they had known how this fear is accentuated if one has experienced a major trauma in an enclosed situation (an accident, a car wreck, sexual abuse, surgery), they would have quickly recognized the possibility that their conscious feelings were fooling them. Perhaps they would have been able to say to themselves, "Maybe deep down I don't really want or need to leave this marriage/this therapy."

Once again we see that one of the most powerful understandings we can come to is how often our conscious feelings lie to us—how our conscious mind is not set up to give us the whole truth. If we can add to this awareness a healthy respect for our punishing intelligence, then we will be on our way to a significantly enhanced self-understanding. And we will find ourselves making fewer bad choices.

CHAPTER EIGHT

Building Victors Instead of Victims

The patient was certain the doctor was wrong and told him so. "I still think I need medication to help my depression. I've been giving it more and more thought," Fred forthrightly told his psychiatrist, Dr. Ballantine. The attorney had been coming for therapy for about two months because of his problems with drinking and now depression.

Fred continued, "I know I said something last session, when we discussed using medication, about people who make their children too dependent. But I was talking about the way my cousin treats his children. I don't feel medication would make me dependent."

Dr. Ballantine listened quietly as his patient continued to talk. But he thought to himself, in a silent "conversation" with Fred, *It is amazing how people just can't hear what they are telling themselves. Last session you told me by your stories that medication was not in your best interests. I predict you'll tell me the same thing again.*

A few minutes later Fred pressured Dr. Ballantine for his opinion on using medication. But Dr. Ballantine put the ball back into Fred's court, asking him to continue exploring the matter. Reluctantly, Fred kept talking. "I know a lot of executives in my position who take antidepressants. A lot of them secretly have drinking problems, too."

Then, seemingly shifting gears, Fred further reported, "I've been having a problem with one particular employee. He just can't take responsibility for his actions and tell the truth. He's overlooking his contribution to the problem."

Dr. Ballantine again thought to himself, *That didn't take long. He connected taking pills to secret drinking. Now he is talking about people who don't perceive themselves accurately, particularly when it comes to being individuals and taking responsibility.* Still, he didn't have enough "evidence" from Fred's mind to present to him yet. His patient's mind would have the deciding vote, and for the doctor to get past the biased jury of Fred's conscious mind was quite a job. *Your deeper intelligence has its work cut out for it,* Dr. Ballantine silently said to Fred.

Dr. Ballantine's strategy paid off quickly as Fred unknowingly began talking about a part of himself he saw in his wife: "She doesn't see how dependent she makes her mother. Her mother is getting older but calls her ten or fifteen times a day at any hour. And my wife does exactly what her mother wants. She won't set limits with her."

After that, Fred made another apparently incidental shift in topics as he talked about an associate whose son had a severe wreck while intoxicated. He thought his partner was to blame because he indulged his son.

Now, with enough evidence on hand, Dr. Ballantine suggested to Fred that while he consciously thought he wanted medication, indirectly he was indicating with a whole string of clues that to use medication would foster dependence or indulgence—as his wife had done with her mother and his colleague with his son. It was important that Fred take responsibility in the seemingly little things in life.

Also, Dr. Ballantine suggested that the unrealized fear

of being entrapped and harmed by close relationships—in this case with Dr. Ballantine—had something to do with Fred wanting to escape by using medication.

Dr. Ballantine was pleased with his presentation to the jury of Fred's mind: With some reluctance, Fred agreed to hold off using medication. And afterward, Fred gave him a positive sign, stating that his business had been doing exceptionally well (meaning, "You are doing a good job, doctor").

BUILDING INTO OTHERS—AND THEY INTO US

Throughout our lifetime, whenever we interact with others in any significant way, they become a part of us. We have an incredible ability to take into our minds key events that create indelible impressions; we internalize them, literally building them into who we are. And the more significant the issue that arises, the more someone *builds into us.*

Two primary building blocks shape our lives—the *words* and the *actions* of others. Unfortunately, it is possible for one message to be built into one level and a second, contradictory message to be built into the deeper level. The contradictions most commonly appear between our words and our actions.

In essence we are always identifying with others. We think of identification as a process that largely takes place in childhood or adolescence, when people are looking for an identity. However, we are never finished people, and we never quit identifying with others—for good or for bad. In his interaction with Dr. Ballantine, Fred was convinced on one level of his mind that the question of whether or not to use medication was a simple, black-and-white issue. However, knowing Fred possessed a much deeper mind,

Dr. Ballantine was careful about what he built into Fred. Deep down, Fred was saying, "If you give me medication, you will build dependency, weakness, and avoidance into me, which is the way I am constructed now—I avoid my problems by using alcohol. But I want to change."

By understanding Fred's unspoken need to face himself, Dr. Ballantine was able to "build into" Fred a much different perception of himself. He was saying to Fred, "You have enough strength to face your problems. You see the fear that is causing you to run away by drinking too much, and deep down you want to overcome it." By not giving in to Fred's request to avoid his deepest fear, Dr. Ballantine was also saying, "I believe you have what it takes to overcome your fear by looking it in the face."

Before we leave our discussion of Fred, I want to briefly answer the question: Can medication have a role in achieving personal healing or wholeness? By facing his pain, Fred could now be whole and not be a slave to his fear. He could master his fear and become more unified, more together as a person. He was arriving at a new level of self-understanding. Many people wonder, though, as did Fred, if such understanding and medication really are mutually exclusive. Can't you use both simultaneously? *I am not proposing that everyone should stop medication.* However, I do believe that medication is a compromise and not an ideal solution, though it may be necessary, hopefully for the short run.

The deeper intelligence teaches that to take medication may help correct a biological imbalance, but on the deepest and largest level of your mind, it always builds dependence into you and deep down you want to be as absolutely independent as possible.

Dependence always creates some avoidance because it denies your ability to conquer a problem yourself. These are consistent messages from the deeper intelligence. This is why many medical patients develop a hatred of medications they must take, or even, for example, of dialysis machines which keep them alive. Certainly we all are dependent on food, water, air, and love, but beyond these limitations, our deepest desire is always to be as independent as possible. You may be thinking, "Well, I take medication and it doesn't bother me." I encourage you to ask yourself which part of your mind really believes that.

(Let me once again be very clear at this point: In no way am I suggesting that everyone who reads this book should not use or should stop his or her medication. I am saying, rather, that medications are frequently used too often or too long. And there are definite psychological side effects to the use of medications that doctors and patients should be cautious about. Unfortunately, there are some people who must take medication indefinitely, a less than ideal arrangement that they must accept.)

WATCHING OUR WORDS

It is also possible, without realizing it, to contradict our words subtly with other words. Joe Theismann, the former professional quarterback, once told the following story about Washington Redskins Coach Joe Gibbs.

At the beginning of the 1981 football season, the players entered the meeting room for the first team gathering of training camp. Coach Gibbs stood in front of the room, and behind him was a huge message on the blackboard: "Win the Super Bowl." Gibbs had sent his team the unmistakable message that his goal, and thus theirs, was to win the championship. Obligingly, the Redskins carried out his will, culminating their sterling season with a victory in the Super Bowl. They had followed their coach's instructions to the letter.

At training camp the next year, on the first day of team meetings, the scene was much the same. Coach Gibbs stood at the front of the room with the blackboard behind him. The simple message this time carried only the slightest change: "Get back to the Super Bowl." Once again that season his players carried out his instructions to the letter: They got back to the Super Bowl. But they did not win. They had not been given clear instructions to do so.[1]

Gibbs almost certainly talked to his team about winning the Super Bowl at various times during the second season. But inadvertently, at an extremely crucial time—when the goals for the year should have been crystal clear—he had given a slightly muddled message. I believe what Gibbs communicated may have determined his team's fate that year. Leaders have incredible power, and their words and communication have far greater power than even they realize.

Another situation where we must be aware of how our words build into people at two levels is the common argument. Typically in an argument, one person insists on one reality and the other person a separate reality. Usually blame and fault-finding are major parts of an argument.

For example, Dean says to Leslie, "You always tell me I am insensitive, but that's because you do things to provoke me."

Leslie responds, "I never provoke you; I only get upset when you are insensitive."

Then Dean says, "You really are hostile, but you won't admit it."

Leslie in turn replies, "See, I told you that you're a brute! You say the cruelest things. I will never trust you."

And the beat goes on.

If we look not only at what is said directly but also at the hidden powerful messages and roles that go along with the direct communication, we see that each person in turn is building predictable negative responses into the other. Both Dean and Leslie assigned each other badness, blame, hostility, and abandonment. Both Dean and Leslie continued attacking, ridiculing, and alienating the other. Both Dean and Leslie demonstrated a lack of humility and a complete lack of ownership or responsibility for what was going wrong. There was no kindness, no understanding, no empathy.

When all of these qualities are being built into you, particularly when your self-control is not good to start with, the perpetuation of an argument is certain. Can you behave any differently than what has been built into you?

The hub of an argument (or any interaction) consists of two people in essence continually modeling or mirroring certain behaviors for the other person. Each in turn internalizes what they see in the mirror of the other, continually reflecting the very behavior they just experienced. Under these conditions, should people really expect anything but misery out of this type of an argument? Dean treats Leslie like she is a jerk, and then Leslie behaves like a jerk, and then Dean is surprised!

The solution to an argument is obvious (though far from easy)—build the other person into the type person you would want to have a disagreement with, if you have to have one. Begin to demonstrate listening, humility, ownership of the problem, and less hostility. The moment you do this you are building something different into the other person. In the midst of the battle you are holding up to them a mirror of a different kind of response, and although they may keep talking, they will see it.

Often, after a time of testing, the other person will begin to reflect your latest building ventures. Then you will see that just as the book of Proverbs says, "A soft answer turns away wrath" (Prov. 15:1 NKJV). Giving a soft answer does not mean you are a wimp. Just the opposite is the case. Only tough people can give soft answers, for only tough people can keep from being overwhelmed by the other person and becoming like them.

One of the most commonly overlooked problems in an argument is that people are arguing on two levels of their mind and don't recognize it. For example, a husband may be insensitive but be largely unaware of it consciously.

Thus, he has unconsciously attacked his wife, which he knows deep down (as we always do), but it's outside of his conscious perception. His wife, feeling attacked, can't distinguish which level of her husband's mind is attacking her but only knows she has just experienced an attack. Her immediate response is to think her husband "intentionally"—consciously—attacked her. Her response might then be a comment similar to this: "You're just like your father, you say mean things." Even though she may be accurately picking up on her husband's behavior, if he is unaware of it (and we are all so prone to block out our faults) then he will, in turn, feel completely attacked and belittled by her comment. At this point, both spouses are then significantly alienated because they have not understood how the mind works.

One of the most commonly overlooked problems in an argument is that people are arguing on two levels of their mind and don't recognize it.

Better if they understood that usually a person blocks out their faults. Then they can begin to learn how to deal with a blind spot in their partner and themselves. The wife would have approached her husband in a much better fashion if she had acknowledged her husband's probable unawareness. This recognition on her part would certainly have helped her do just that. If, simultaneously, the husband had acknowledged just how great our potential is for being unaware of our communications, he would have been far more able to comprehend his wife's response, even if it was overly hostile.

141

All too often couples are arguing over blind spots they are picking up on in each other without ever realizing their spouse is completely blind to what he or she has done. Thus, one partner is prone to think that the other is consciously lying when their spouse doesn't immediately own what they have done. Acknowledging how great the potential is for self-deception can be of enormous help in derailing hostile patterns of interacting. Also, this self-deception issue cuts both ways and any spouse who is hurt by the other can greatly profit by seriously considering that they themselves could have either overreacted or possibly provoked their spouse. This means more than a person just checking out their feelings to make sure they haven't secretly contributed to the problem but attempting to live by the principles the deeper intelligence suggests.

Another major hurdle to overcome in an argument is self-righteousness. Many times we feel justified in fighting, in retaliating because we have been "wronged." Many times we are unconsciously looking to be wronged in order to express our anger. If we want to know the truth, this is a major part of every serious argument.

Most of the time the real issue in arguments is not *what* we are arguing about but *that* we argue. Honest disagreement is rarely a problem in relationships, but ridicule is.

Most of the time the real issue in arguments is not what we are arguing about but that we argue.

The bottom line in all our interactions is that, generally

speaking, we reap what we sow. In light of knowing how greatly others identify with us in the way we treat them, I must underscore the importance of Jesus' remarkable understanding of human nature and His counsel to us in what has become known as the Golden Rule: In essence, "Treat others as you want to be treated." The question before us is, What traits are we building into those around us as we interact with them—this day, this hour, this minute? Are we building into others the qualities through our words and actions that will make them victors in facing the hurdles of life, or are we preparing them for the role of victim?

ROLE CREATION: PLAYING PSYCHOLOGICAL "HOT POTATO"

Because we are human, many times we secretly attempt to build into others painful emotional states that we possess, thinking (subconsciously) that we can rid ourselves of our pain by giving it to another person. Often others, particularly through their actions, try to create in us a role that they are trying to shed in order to assume the safer, less painful role of a victim. The following story from psychotherapy highlights this very common but subtle maneuver.

It was one of Dr. Rita Larson's favorite times of the day. After three hours of intensive psychotherapy, she always took a thirty-minute break to open her mail, return phone calls, and relax for a few minutes before seeing the final three patients of her long day.

The first letter today was personal—handwritten. Dr. Larson recognized the last name as that of her patient Louisa. Experience told her that any letter wasn't a good sign. She quickly recalled that Louisa had cancelled her last session, leaving a clipped message on the answering machine.

Dr. Larson opened the letter, and Louisa's words leaped off the page, barely disguising a deep sense of rage: "Dear Dr. Larson: Since you didn't care enough to return my phone call when I called to cancel my session, I am terminating my therapy with you."

Dr. Larson thought back. *The only message on my answering machine was that Louisa was canceling for this week.* Dr. Larson had known at the time that the most likely reason for Louisa to miss was that she was dealing with powerful issues. Nevertheless, Dr. Larson could only assume that from the message that there wasn't a crisis and Louisa was simply canceling her session and would return for her appointment next week. *Did I miss something in her phone message?* Dr. Larson wondered.

The letter continued: "You also know that I have been having financial problems and wanted to discontinue therapy. You have been ignoring my requests. You wanted me to keep coming when I really couldn't afford to. You just weren't listening to me. There have been a few other times when I tried to talk to you on the telephone between sessions when I was upset, and you always tried to keep the conversation short—wanting me to discuss matters in our next session."

Dr. Larson remembered those incidents. Each time, in the session following the phone call, Louisa's deeper intelligence had revealed the importance of dealing with important issues during a session and not on the phone.

Dr. Larson continued reading: "You must have too many patients, and I no longer will be any trouble to you because I am no longer your patient. Please send me a bill for what I owe you. Also, please do not try to contact me. I am not interested in talking with you. Sincerely yours, Louisa."

Dr. Larson was stunned. For almost a year she had met with Louisa on a weekly basis; never had she experienced this type of behavior coming from her. Dr. Larson thought back to Louisa's last session, and soon things began to fall into place. Louisa had been at one of those crucial points— a life-enhancing moment, if she would have allowed herself to develop through it.

What had been coming into focus was the real reason why Louisa always selected very destructive men (she'd had three bad marriages). In the last session she had talked about her last husband in particular, how he had made her his victim; how he repeatedly had beaten her when he was abusing alcohol; how he eventually had ruined them financially. She also had described this ex-husband as someone who was selfish and avoided uncomfortable subjects. He wasn't willing to pay the price to face himself, which he desperately needed to do. She knew he must be abusing alcohol because he was afraid of something. He was like her Uncle Ralph, who was addicted to pain medication.

Also in the last session, Louisa had mentioned the medication she was getting from her family doctor for panic symptoms. Then she had brought up discontinuing therapy because money was tight. (Of course, money was tight, but her deeper intelligence made plain that that was not the primary issue. Louisa had an excellent job and had options for obtaining the money if she really wanted to. Money is often a large issue in therapy, because it is one way the patient can powerfully express hidden issues. But this is a discussion for another time and place.)

Dr. Larson remembered pointing out to Louisa that the medication she was receiving from her doctor was getting in the way; it was creating a sense of addiction in her life that caused her to block out the real fear behind the pain. Dr. Larson also suggested that Louisa herself was saying that now was the time to come off her medicine, face her fear, and continue with therapy at this crucial time, despite the financial hardship—in short, to pay the price of knowing herself. Privately, Dr. Larson knew that she wasn't trying to hold on to Louisa. She had a busy schedule and could easily fill Louisa's place.

At that point Louisa had talked about how she missed her mother, who had died a few years before. Her mom had done everything for her. Then Louisa mentioned the time she had had a frightening car wreck and was all alone. Her mother hadn't been there to comfort her. She didn't want to go through that again.

The session had ended on that note. Dr. Larson had realized that Louisa was terrified about facing her real fears—fears of being damaged if she allowed herself to be a real individual in a close relationship; fears that were being accentuated when a third party (like her family) wasn't around to rescue her or when medications were not there to block out the fear. Her own words were telling her this and, as usual, Dr. Larson had been careful not to say anything more than Louisa had said.

Typically, she had found a way to assume the familiar role of victim in order to obscure a potentially more frightening part of herself.

Once more Dr. Larson read Louisa's letter, this time in light of her last session. Everything began to come together much more clearly. Louisa obviously had been very anxious as she approached her deepest fear. Now she was choosing to allow it to continue to control and wreck her life rather than face it. Louisa had agreed to come off her medication, at the suggestion of her own deeper intelligence, which would enable her to see herself much more clearly. But, obviously, she had grown anxious, missed the session because "she was sick," and used an unfortunate incident to stop her therapy. Typically, she had found a way to assume the familiar role of victim in order to obscure a potentially more frightening part of herself.

At this crucial point in her therapy, Louisa had become very frightened of Dr. Larson because she was approaching the deepest fear which controlled her life. Now Louisa wanted to destroy her therapy in different ways by destroying the boundaries of therapy. Without clear boundaries, she would not have a clear therapy and thus her fears would be obscured. Missing a session, wanting to stop therapy, wanting medications, and wanting contact with her therapist outside the boundaries of her session all were ways of destroying the boundaries of the one-to-one relationship—the very boundaries which could eventually bring healing to her. Louisa was behaving just like her ex-husband, who destroyed a nurturing one-to-one relationship with her. In her own words, in the last session and in the letter, Louisa told Dr. Larson why she was doing all this: She couldn't afford the therapy. Yet her right brain, her deeper intelligence, was saying that Louisa felt a true one-to-one relationship would be too threatening, that she would have to pay too big a price. Because in one-to-one relationships people got damaged like two cars that ran into each other.

Louisa also was terrified of her own anger, so much so that she had to express it indirectly through a letter and not in person. This helped explain why she chose such destructive men. If they expressed their anger, she could blame them and wouldn't have to face up to the parts of herself that frightened her and caused her to feel guilty. This was behind the letter to Dr. Larson canceling her therapy: She needed to express her anger and yet avoid doing it directly.

Clearly Louisa's letter was designed to make her therapist feel accused, labeled, insensitive, and cruel. Despite Dr. Larson's efforts to help her patient, Louisa had turned on her suddenly. Dr. Larson felt betrayed, hurt, and a bit angry.

Then it dawned on Dr. Larson: *All the things that Louisa felt in her marriage, she has just made me feel—and she hasn't had to own any of it. She has just given me a large part of herself—uncomfortable feelings that she has— without even knowing it.* All the powerful emotions Louisa herself struggled with, Dr. Larson was now confronting—being a victim, feeling helpless, taken advantage of financially, and being made to feel badly as the guilty party.

Dr. Larson thought sadly, *On top of all this, Louisa has managed to convince herself she has been victimized by me. In the back of her mind, she even knows she is refusing to see what she is doing, as she talked about her husband not wanting to know what he was doing.* Louisa had obviously done much of the same thing in her marriage—sought out and enhanced her husband's role as a victimizer. The truth was, she was looking to be victimized, to avoid a true one-to-one and her fear of closeness because of fearing her own aggression. Unconsciously, she chose people who would fulfill the roles she needed them to play. Even when Dr. Larson attempted to avoid the role, somehow Louisa created circumstances to have her perform it anyway.

Dr. Larson had just been the recipient of a *role creation.* In the essentially neutral but nurturing environment she was experiencing, Louisa eventually had to cast Dr. Larson in a role that Louisa thought she needed her to play. At a crucial moment, Louisa had made Dr. Larson into her victim and was blind to having done so.

People *create roles* in others initially for two reasons—to share their pain and at the same time to avoid their pain. (Deep down, we also want to resolve our pain.) Louisa did both to Dr. Larson. First she shared her pain, making Dr. Larson feel victimized as she did. Then she tried to avoid her anger by making Dr. Larson feel the anger Louisa was uncomfortable expressing directly herself. The ultimate reason people create rules for others is to keep someone in a negative role to avoid an intimate one-to-one.

People create roles in others for two reasons—to share their pain and at the same time to avoid their pain.

Creating a role for someone to play happens every day in almost any situation we might encounter. If we understand that our deeper intelligence is aware of it and wants to draw our attention to it for the sake of enhancing our relationships, we will be much better off. We will become much more open to our effects on others, as well as recognize more clearly the pressures others place on us.

Louisa is not alone in seeking out a victim role. It is an amazingly common role we all, in fact, assume at certain moments. The victim role is enticing because it enables us to secretly express our aggression (accuse the other), hide our guilt ("you are the bad one, not I"), avoid responsibility, and keep our distance. It is an easy and natural role—we seem born for the part. The only problem is that the ultimate payoff is high: We continually deny who we really are and also deny ourselves the pleasure of intimacy.

A relinquishing of this ever-present but self-defeating role would have major benefits for our society as a whole, as well as for us as individuals. Just think of the benefits to our nation if more people took responsibility for who they are and denied themselves the temporary pleasure of the victim role and instead became victors in facing both their internal and external problems.

149

Throughout our lifetime, others are creating roles for us and we for them. If we can begin to have less faith in what our feelings tell us (about what has happened in a particular situation) and understand how inclined we are to cast or to be cast into certain roles, then we can consider that we may have made a significant contribution to any role we find unacceptable.

PART THREE

Using Your
Deeper Intelligence

CHAPTER NINE

The Deeper Intelligence and Marriage

I trust you have begun to sense some of the challenges that the deeper intelligence presents to our normal ways of looking at the world. Already we have gained new information about relationships: The heightened prominence and power of one-to-one relationships, the potential for powerful disruptions of these crucial relationships by subtle boundary modifications, and the degree to which we fear the stability we long for in our primary relationships. Now I want to look more closely at several of our most important life-giving, one-to-one relationships, starting with the one that is generally regarded as the most important human relationship in adulthood—marriage.

* * *

The solitary woman sat quietly, surrounded by towering oaks and pine trees on the edge of the woods. Rene was virtually motionless, except for occasionally moving a hand to lift her coffee cup. Encompassed by the forest and the nurturing sounds of nature, this was the place she came when she wanted to escape or think. Today it was to think—and to recover from the jolt she'd had in psychotherapy that morning.

It had only been her third session with her therapist, Dr. Smithey, and already they had delved into some important issues—but these weren't the issues she had anticipated. She wondered, *Am I actually a different person than I'd thought?*

Rene had reached out to this therapist for help when she'd come to the end of her rope in dealing with her husband, Stewart. Stewart's abusive, shaming tirades were driving her up a wall, and she was so frustrated she didn't know what to do. She wasn't even sure she wanted to stay in the marriage.

From the beginning of therapy Dr. Smithey had quietly rebuffed her attempts to solicit advice and guidance. This had puzzled her, because that's what she thought therapists were supposed to do. But at one point Dr. Smithey had conveyed the idea that to help her understand herself was the most help he could offer, and that would shed light on her marriage. Rene had been hoping instead that the doctor would recommend some helpful book that perhaps she could pass along to her husband. But the therapist had kept telling her, "Just keep talking so we—you and I—can understand your situation."

It felt a bit strange, but Rene was so desperate for help she was willing to try anything. She trusted the doctor who had referred her to Dr. Smithey; she remembered his words to her after he'd made the referral: "He will help you understand your situation. Trust him—there may be some difficult moments." That was why she'd been willing to go back for a third session, the one that had really shook her up.

She remembered telling Dr. Smithey of her frustration with Stewart's outbursts and also how he openly flirted at times with other women, even though she knew it was harmless. Nevertheless, it had led to a lot of antagonism in their marriage. Rene had also mentioned asking Stewart to come to her appointment with her that day, but he had refused. Rene then had suggested to Dr. Smithey that he call their pastor, who had counseled both her and her husband in the recent past. Perhaps their pastor could give him some helpful information about Stewart. She had mentioned that, of course, she was open to whatever was her part in their problems. But Dr. Smithey hadn't responded to her suggestion immediately, so she'd just kept talking as he'd asked her to do.

That was when she had talked about her first marriage. Her husband then was an alcoholic who abused her, and one night she thought he was going to kill her. That reminded her of the tirades her father used to have, and she remembered a night when she had witnessed him severely beating her mother. It seemed Stewart was like all the other men in her life. Rene didn't think she could trust any of them. Before she and Stewart had started attending church and trying to get their lives together, Stewart had had a long history of affairs; he just couldn't be tied down. Now he was better, though he still flirted.

Rene still wanted Dr. Smithey to talk with their pastor, since he had witnessed some of Stewart's flirtations. Besides, Stewart would listen to their pastor if Dr. Smithey wanted to make some suggestions to him. That was the moment Dr. Smithey had made his shocking comment to her:

"I think you are telling me that if I talk to your pastor, it would be like a spouse who couldn't be loyal to you. Now, the question is, why would a part of you want me to bring a third party into our work here, when it's not really in your best interests? I think you're asking me this because, as much as you want solid relationships, you also fear them and unknowingly undermine them. This fear stems from previous one-to-one relationships which were hurtful. So now, unknowingly, you create distance in one-to-ones, just as you're doing here. I believe you must be doing the same thing in your marriage without realizing it, and contributing to your own suffering. Part of you is trying to help you realize this so you can have a better marriage."

It had been shocking to think that she was having a real part in her marital problems. Rene did admit that she *had* suggested bringing her husband and her pastor into the session; she just hadn't thought it was all that important.

To Dr. Smithey, though, the place where her mind went at that point was even more important. For some reason she began talking about the time she went swimming in the river as a young ten-year-old with her cousin, Ralph. She'd nearly drowned that day. She remembered clinging to Ralph after she'd taken in too much water. The experience had been terrifying.

At the end of the session Dr. Smithey told her, "The stories you've told us today are your mind's way of saying these are the issues you have to deal with, issues which must be affecting your marriage. Deep down you've come to believe that a one-to-one relationship is dangerous, like swimming in deep waters. You feel you will be in over your head. That's why you want to escape the one-to-one by bringing in a third party. You must overcome this fear of a one-to-one to have the marriage you want. And remember, these are your ideas. I am just repeating them back to you, so you can see them."

Now, under the trees in the woods, Rene continued to replay the confusing session in her mind. She had many questions: Was she actually that much out of touch with herself? Could it be she really was like her husband, having problems with loyalty in their relationship? Was she actually afraid of a truly intimate relationship? All these notions seemed so bizarre.

If Rene wanted a strong marriage but tended secretly to undermine it, perhaps her husband wasn't the only one at fault. Maybe she was doing more than she'd thought to affect the relationship. If that was the case, then the two of them had a greater problem than they realized. If Rene had understood that, perhaps she might have begun to look more seriously for ways she was supporting Stewart's tirades. For instance, she made subtle maneuvers, such as enabling Stewart to be verbally abusive by not setting limits with him; she secretly encouraged his subtle involvement with a third party (by involving third parties in the marriage herself, like their pastor); and then she criticized him for doing so, or provoked him to anger in various ways and discounted her own contribution to the third-party involvement.

Unknowingly, Rene was living out one of the most common distancing techniques people struggle with in marriage: She was setting up her spouse to play a role—the angry one—and then complaining about it when he did. Secretly, Rene was expressing disguised aggressiveness (what is often called passive aggression) by being careless with the family budget, keeping a sloppy house, or repeatedly overworking and being too tired for intimacy. She needed to keep Stewart at a distance, and these were highly-effective maneuvers to accomplish that goal. Yet she was completely blind to the meaning of her behavior.

Of course Stewart had a problem with his anger and with his own fear of one-to-ones; but Rene was making a significant contribution to their problems. To outward appearances, it appeared that Stewart was almost exclusively "the bad guy," when the truth of the matter was far different. Rene was heavily invested in Stewart's wearing the black hat in the family, secretly encouraging Stewart to take the negative role of the "bad one" or "the guilty one." Often we encourage others in a role to express hidden parts of ourselves: Rene wanted Stewart to be the angry, guilty person.

Her left brain was not helping matters. She was convinced that virtually all of the problem was Stewart's and was proposing false solutions. Rather than helping Stewart she was modeling disloyalty, encouraging others to label her husband just as she was doing, and contributing to his anger. Her left brain, controlled by her punishing intelligence, was winning out over her deeper intelligence, which recognized a far better way. Rene—frozen in her limited left-brain awareness—was depriving herself of the very marriage she wanted.

But any therapist who did not listen to the deeper intelligence probably would have overlooked the most helpful cure Rene needed: to hear in her own words how she was exactly like her husband, in her own way.

Think about what might have happened if Rene had seen a therapist who did not appreciate the deeper intelligence. Many therapists would have accepted her left-brain description of what was going on—that her husband was the main problem and she needed to learn how to deal with him. Such therapists likely would have advised her on how to handle him; some might even have encouraged her to leave him. Others might have pointed out to her how she encouraged her husband's tirades by not setting limits with him. But any therapist who did not listen to the deeper intelligence probably would have overlooked the most helpful cure Rene needed: to hear in her own words how she was exactly like her husband, in her own way.

Only by being able to hear the deeper intelligence would a therapist understand the importance of her actions, which were subtle but clear ways of destroying intimacy and destabilizing the marriage.

The deeper intelligence helps reveal how challenging a marriage is because it touches on our deepest-seated fear—fear of intimacy. This powerful and universal anxiety comes into play more significantly in marriage than in any other human relationship. The dread associated with closeness (security anxiety) is a primary issue in marriage. What must be overcome is the fear that we will be abandoned, judged, or destroyed in a tight one-to-one relationship (or that we will do the same to our partner). Knowing what the real issues are will help us overcome the many obstacles to a meaningful marriage.

AVOIDING A ONE-TO-ONE—MARRIAGE STYLE

As I have mentioned previously, there are three basic ways of avoiding a one-to-one relationship, and they all come into play in a marriage. The first way is to directly avoid the one-to-one—to leave the marriage. Obviously, divorce is the most clear-cut form of withdrawal from a marriage. But avoidance also can take place while a couple remains married. Each spouse can distance through outside activities (work, hobbies, sports, club activities) or by simply withdrawing emotionally. Anger and criticism, which ultimately assign a spouse a negative role, are perhaps the most common ways of unconsciously creating distance in a marriage.

A second way of avoiding a one-to-one in marriage is by encouraging, consciously or unconsciously, a third party to come between the spouses. Third parties can be people (children, parents, friends, a lover) or activities (a hobby, a job, or volunteer involvement). In many cases an affair is not what it looks to be, either to the partners or from the outside; usually the people involved never understand their true motives. I believe that at the deepest level of their minds people become involved in affairs not out of love or even lust, but out of fear. In fact, the fear that must be overcome in any marriage—fear of intimacy—is enormous. In almost every marriage, at least one partner at some point will experience the pressure to destroy the clear boundaries of this most sacred relationship by an affair, or by drawing closer to a friend or a child rather than the spouse.

I believe that at the deepest level of their minds people become involved in affairs not out of love or even lust, but out of fear.

A third way of dramatically altering the one-to-one in marriage is by both parties giving up their distinctive personalities. In Rene and Stewart's case, Stewart was saying through his aggression, "I don't really want you to be a person, so I will control you." And Rene obliged him when she became passive and didn't stand up to him when he was abusive. Only another individual can provide consequences for someone when that someone mistreats him or her. By not setting limits with Stewart, Rene was "enabling" his misbehavior, as well as expressing a hidden part of herself.

A recent movie, *Mrs. Doubtfire,* captures many of these secret distancing techniques that we are so prone to develop in marriage. In the movie, Robin Williams portrays an irresponsible husband who is loved by his children but disliked by an angry but responsible wife. When the couple separates, remarkable changes take place in both. The husband becomes responsible, the wife less angry and more loving, and they get along far better than they had as a couple.

In short, once they were out of the marriage, they were free to give up their distancing techniques. I believe one of the subtle messages of the movie is that spouses are under great pressure to create negative roles for each other. Prior to their separation, both spouses were caught up in assigning the other a certain negative role—in essence blaming the spouse for the problem and, as well, caught up in certain individual personality patterns. Both tendencies, blaming and refusing to change annoying behaviors, were a hidden agenda each spouse used to keep the other at a distance.

UNIQUE MOMENTS IN MARRIAGE

There are crucial times in marriage when we see with more clarity the great pressure a one-to-one exerts, when circumstances force the one-to-one to be closer or more clearly defined. One such time is when a couple's children reach adolescence. Adolescents often attempt to divide and conquer their parents. However, as adolescents pull away from their parents, a vacuum is created in the family relational structure that puts pressure on the couple to draw closer. At that point, many times unknowingly, this uncomfortable pressure can lead a couple to opt for even *more* distancing. The couple can easily fool themselves into thinking the only problem is the turmoil caused by the adolescent, when it is at least equally their fear of closeness with each other. (This effect increases when the children leave home.)

Constantly throughout a marriage, both partners have to deal with the pressure to reinforce certain negative roles for their partner—roles which create distance and allow both persons to hide a part of themselves in another. As

Rene reinforced Stewart's aggression and hid a part of herself (her own anger) in him, she grew to dislike him more and kept him at a distance. Stewart, by locating his unacceptable dependency and helplessness in Rene, created distance in exactly the same way. If both had begun to understand they were more like each other than they realized, they could have had empathy for each other and enhanced their closeness instead of undermining it.

There are crucial times in marriage when we see with more clarity the great pressure a one-to-one exerts, when circumstances force the one-to-one to be closer or more clearly defined.

It is true that opposites attract, but it is also true that a marriage cannot be so simply defined. Because we are all much more alike than we realize, deep down the issues we struggle with in a marriage are very similar. There is always a hidden agenda, a hidden strategy to distance each other which must be overcome.

THE POWER OF ONE

As a therapist, I never cease to be amazed at the power one partner in a marriage possesses to change the marriage for the good. In numerous instances I have witnessed one spouse, completely exclusive of the other party, begin to deal with personal issues in individual therapy and then make significant changes for good in the marriage.

The reason one partner can have such a powerful effect

on the other is because of the ongoing *building* or *identification* process that goes on in a marriage. As we have discussed previously, we are constantly building into each other. If, for example, Rene would come to terms with her own anger and her inclination to push Stewart into an angry role, she could begin building different traits in him. And if she does, she will receive different responses from Stewart.

Marriage is both a left-brain and a right-brain relationship. Usually we know, or can fairly easily determine, the left-brain aspects of our marriage. But we also have a right brain, and this powerful part of our mind has a major voice in our decisions and personality patterns. Here it is that we have a lot to learn.

Marriage is both a left-brain and a right-brain relationship.

Too many times I have seen one spouse in psychotherapy complain about the other spouse's behavior without recognizing her attempt to elicit the same behavior from me. (For example, if Dr. Smithey had gone along with Rene's suggestion to include a third party in their therapy, he would have been disloyal to her.) This means only one thing—the patient is subtly reinforcing and actually seeking in her spouse the very behavior that disturbs her. The reason for this behavior *in every case* is a deep and abiding fear of a true one-to-one relationship and, as well, a fear of owning one's powerful emotions.

Not infrequently I work with people whose spiritual life is a big part of their identity. Even so, I have yet to see a single spouse who deep down has seriously considered the remarkable counsel of Jesus to remove the log in one's own eye before worrying about the speck in a neighbor's eye. Not one has said, "You know, the very fault I find with my spouse could be the identical flaw I possess also." But the deeper intelligence quickly understands this reality and attempts to point out to people that often when they are talking about others, they are talking about themselves in some way. And those who accept that the mind works this way make the most progress, because they are the best listeners.

This saying of Jesus—that we may have the same problem or flaw we can see in someone else—should be our standard, both in and out of therapy. As we have seen, there are crucial moments in every psychotherapy when a patient is faced with the option of staying in a healthy one-to-one or avoiding it—distancing himself from the very relationship he wants. Many such moments occur in marriage (as well as in our other relationships, particularly between parents and adolescents). Just as patients (or therapists) all too often unknowingly choose distance over a committed one-to-one, marital partners tend to make the same choice.

Learning to expect these crucial moments—moments offering great potential for change—and having a strategy to handle them can pay huge dividends by producing a much more intimate marriage.

The key moment in marital discord comes when both partners must decide if they are going to continue externalizing a problem onto their mate or learn to reconcile the relationship by building healthier traits into the partner. Blaming begets blaming and more distance. But understanding, containment, rising above immediate feelings, forgiveness, and assuming responsibility undercut negative role creations and distancing in marriage.

These crucial moments appear throughout marriage. We will not win all of these battles to be a healthy reconciler; but the more we win, the better our marriage will be. And the more we win, the fewer battles we will have. Learning to expect these crucial moments—moments offering great potential for change—and having a strategy to handle them can pay huge dividends by producing a much more intimate marriage.

BENEFITTING FROM THE DEEPER MIND

Of course not everyone is a therapist or can participate in therapy, so what should we do with deeper mind communications if we aren't professionally trained? Are they really of any benefit to us?

These communications offer a very powerful starting place. If we can just begin to grasp how often we create or reinforce negative roles in our spouse, we will become much better listeners—to ourselves and our wives and husbands. If we can grasp how often we fail to realize the meaning of our own words or actions—our true motives—then incredible growth can take place. Furthermore, if we can begin to see each other as allies who desire insight, rather than as enemies, then we've made our first huge step.

If we honor our partners, then we undercut the ever-present tendency to resort to mutual blaming where both parties are simply using each other as human waste baskets to get rid of unacceptable parts of their personalities. And if we can begin to appreciate how truly difficult

165

it is to establish an honest-to-goodness marriage and how we all tend to distance ourselves from our mates, we will realize the challenge before us. Then we will have more empathy for each other and begin to distrust some of the conscious lies we tell ourselves about the problem areas in our marriage.

If we truly make an effort to know our right brain—to know our complete self—we will live by the code recommended by the deeper intelligence. We will be willing to consider that every word we say may be a part of us. And we will become willing to ask ourselves at any moment, particularly those moments in our marriages when our feelings tell us differently, "Am I at this moment talking about the log in my own eye?"

By understanding how our minds work, then we all might begin to walk a little more softly and to carry a little stick, not a big one. This awareness gives us a better chance than ever of stabilizing our marriage.

By understanding how our minds work, then we all might begin to walk a little more softly and to carry a little stick, not a big one.

Marriage and family are the bedrock of society, and too many people are walking away from their bedrock, their foundation, for the wrong reasons and to their detriment. Tragically, many walk away from marriages that deep down they really don't want to leave, as their deeper intelligence would reveal if allowed to do so.

The deeper intelligence brings to us a new understanding of the ever-challenging dynamics of marriage.

And when we begin to understand how our minds are constructed and how they communicate, we can begin to see all sorts of exciting possibilities for relational healing, restoration, and growth.

CHAPTER TEN

The Deeper Intelligence and Parenting

As a fall breeze swept across the front porch where they sat, Linda and Roland were deep in conversation. They had been stunned by the behavior of their only child, twelve-year-old Ashley. She had always been an agreeable, compliant child. So learning that she and some friends had skipped school and gone to the mall was a shock. Fortunately, another mother had caught the girls and would bring Ashley home soon. Linda and Roland were completely puzzled, but they knew they had to confront Ashley.

Linda had attended a seminar on the deeper intelligence and learned that every child tests boundaries at some point. Nevertheless, both she and her husband were concerned about Ashley's behavior.

When Ashley arrived, she walked in looking sheepish but also shocked at herself. Roland began by asking her what she had to say. Ashley replied, "Nothing," and fell silent. Then Linda tried to get some answers. She was met with a consistent response: "I don't know—I just did it."

Despite her parents continued efforts, and even though Ashley eventually became tearful and repentant, she did

168

not give them any real answers as to why she had behaved as she had. There had been no other signs of behavior problems. Knowing that adolescents often can't consciously explain their behavior, and also out of desperation, Linda decided to try something creative.

So she asked Ashley to make up a story—any story that came to mind—and explained to her that sometimes stories could be helpful in working out misunderstandings. Ashley was reluctant at first; but being in big trouble, she was not in a position to argue.

Ashley told a story of a cat who had no brothers or sisters and had gone out to play. The cat jumped over a fence near his house and walked for a long time by himself but couldn't find any other cat at home. Finally, the cat ran into another cat and they played in the woods, climbing trees and running. Soon the other cat had to go home, leaving the first cat to play by himself.

So the cat decided to go swimming for a while in a nearby creek. Sitting by the creek reminded the cat of the old neighborhood where he had lived and how there were a lot of cats that played together there, swimming and climbing. Finally the cat decided to go home but got lost and scared. After a long while, the cat found the fence he had climbed and followed it back home.

When Ashley finished her story, she sat quietly in her chair in the family room. Both parents immediately were struck by the stark loneliness in her story. Soon some pieces of the puzzle began to come together for them. Linda recalled how Ashley had been upset recently when some other girls—her "friends"—had ganged up on her and ridiculed her new haircut.

Linda and Roland asked Ashley if anything was going on in her life to make her feel lonely. Ashley didn't respond directly, but she did mention several recent incidents in which she had been left out by her friends. It was a new school year, and her best friend from last year was not in any of her classes. There had been two times when groups of girls didn't invite her to their spend-the-night parties.

Later, when Linda and Roland reflected privately on Ashley's story, they realized several other triggers for her behavior, each having to do with being left out. The family had moved to this neighborhood two years ago from another town, and Ashley had been in a different school both years. Now a new school year was starting and Ashley again was faced with finding her "place." Her story had contained a thought of an old neighborhood, and they realized how that memory would have been intensified by the new school year.

Linda, through her understanding of human development, also realized Ashley might be beginning to think about how she would soon be in high school and then in a few years leaving for college. The recent change to the next level in school had almost certainly prompted Ashley to realize her separation down the road from her family.

Linda and Roland soon appreciated in a new way that Ashley was dealing with all kinds of issues surrounding separation. Knowing how capable the human mind is, they saw in a new way how richly the deeper intelligence can communicate in everyday life. They certainly intended to discipline their daughter; but now they better understood the pressure Ashley had been under and her recent behavior. They felt sure Ashley had joined a group of girls in skipping school because of a desperate need to belong, triggered by a number of stresses. She also was probably frightened by her emerging independence, and through her misbehavior was requesting a redefinition of strong boundaries. Now they could discipline her with compassion and be more attuned to her needs.

PARENTING WITH THE DEEPER MIND

The deeper intelligence makes its appearance in everyday life just as it does in psychotherapy. Usually we can best hear it at those moments when there is an extremely clear-cut situation on the table. The key to understanding Ashley involved a search through the events, to find the trigger behind her actions.

The deeper intelligence makes its appearance in everyday life just as it does in psychotherapy. Usually we can best hear it at those moments when there is an extremely clear-cut situation on the table.

As Ashley's parents approached her problem, they did so with the intent of handling her misbehavior in the way that would best help her to manage the difficult challenges of growing up. Not all parents manage the upheavals life brings quite so well. And when they don't, the effect on their children can be powerful—in a negative direction. If instead of listening and seeking to understand Ashley's situation Linda and Roland had laid on a guilt trip and shamed her, the bridge between parents and child would have begun to weaken. When carried to an extreme (and over time), this can help spawn *serious* teen problems, such as premarital sex, pregnancy, or alcohol and substance abuse.

Psychotherapy and listening to the deeper intelligence provide us with a remarkable opportunity to better understand parenting, because in many ways the two processes are similar. Ashley's parents were successful in their handling of their daughter's problems because they attempted to listen to the immediate voice of the deeper intelligence as well as operate by its clear principles. Just what did they observe?

Psychotherapy and listening to the deeper intelligence provide us with a remarkable opportunity to better understand parenting, because in many ways the two processes are similar.

First, Ashley's parents recognized her behavior as a request for help. Although they didn't understand what was happening, they attempted to listen to her, even to the point of having to initiate creative ways of listening to her communicate. When their own understanding was not enough, they looked to her for guidance, hoping she would lead them to understanding her.

Roland and Linda handled the stress in the family straightforwardly, confronting the problem rather than avoiding it. And Ashley was fortunate to have two parents committed to managing the boundaries of their family. Obviously, the school was an extension of the home, and when Ashley violated the school's rules, she was also violating her parents' framework. Roland and Linda quickly made sure Ashley knew the boundaries were back in place.

We see other healthy ways these parents responded. When confronted with a somewhat major incident, they successfully contained their frustration; they offered their daughter even more stability when they demonstrated a unified front as parents; and they did not resort to hostility and berating, but instead opted for a matter-of-fact approach toward their daughter. In doing this, they validated her in a powerful way, saying to her clearly that she was important enough to them to be understood. They taught her that the way to work through problems is to talk things out, particularly when everyone is confused.

PARENTING AND THERAPY HAVE MUCH IN COMMON

A parent and a therapist deal with very similar issues. Both must know the needs that arise in a one-to-one and therefore must understand the "rules" involved in such a relationship.

First, both parents and therapists must have an understanding of *the importance of boundaries*. To do this, parents must know where boundaries lie. And they must recognize not only that the boundaries they set *will* be tested, but they must recognize *when* they are being tested as well (more on this in a moment).

Yet parents must likewise understand the tremendous need all people have for freedom. To do this, they can borrow some principles from therapists. For example, in psychotherapy, a therapist encourages tremendous freedom in the patient by encouraging him to be himself, explore his mind, and express himself. The therapist attempts to help the patient attain a balance between freedom and self-control, and while permitting this great freedom, he is constantly attuned to make sure his patient doesn't step outside the boundaries he needs. A therapist is constantly listening and observing for clues that the patient is violating certain boundaries that the patient's right brain knows.

Also, like therapists, parents can be confident that somehow their child will attempt to let them know when he is moving outside the boundaries he needs. We've already mentioned two examples of this. The teenager

Brad gave hints that he really didn't need to play in a rock band, and the college student Slade, whose father overindulged him, also indicated indirectly that he needed stronger, clearer boundaries.

Thus, just as therapists must understand how they affect their patients—that is, building into them on two levels—so parents must know how they are having a major impact on their children on two levels. Parents must continually be aware that their kids have two levels to their personality, both of which are tremendously affected by the parents' personalities. In fact, a parent's greatest influence on his child is often hidden. For example, just as a patient can minimize an important action on the part of a therapist, a child can discount an action or communication from a parent. One conscious example is discipline— virtually no child sees the importance of it initially but the deeper intelligence cries out for it.

There is one more striking similarity between parents and therapists in the important role they play both as *stabilizers* in the lives of others. The stabilizing presence that parents play with their children is usually a thankless job. The main feedback that securely held children give to parents is much like the feedback patients give to therapists: They simply function significantly better.

Sometimes children from a stable home have significant behavior problems during adolescence and constantly challenge their boundaries. It may be a few years before these kids appear to have incorporated the stability of their parents. Remember the proverb: "Train up a child in the way he should go / And when he is old he will not depart from it" (Prov. 22:6 NKJV). However, when an adolescent appears out of control, it is always wise to take a real look at the dynamics of what is going on in the home at that time.

Parents need to know that one of the most important things they do for their children may seem to go unappreciated, often for years. It also can help to know that children often fight the very stability they need.

The good news for parents is that no matter how much they have failed their kids, every day is a new opportunity to build into their children what they need deep down. Parents can begin to build health and stability at any time they choose, because of the phenomenal ability of the mind to want to correct a defect; indeed, it never stops seeking wholeness.

Thus, another striking benefit of dealing with the deeper intelligence is that it always offers us incredible hope. It never gives up in its determination to help us find the right path as people and as parents.

THE SPECIAL CHALLENGES OF ADOLESCENCE

Teenagers occupy such a special place in life's spectrum that they could be compared to a special season of the year. If our retirement years can be seen as the autumn of our life, then surely the teenage years are like the winds of March in an unpredictable spring. And for many parents it seems adolescents require a special understanding.

Parents must remember, the mind wants the best for itself, and deep down teenagers are no different from anyone else. Somewhere in their minds they are inclined to listen to their parents because they need the insight and stability they have to offer.

175

Teenagers often communicate in indirect ways—by actions such as withdrawal, or by role creation. An example of role creation occurs when they are not sure they are needed, so they want their parents to feel the same uncertainty. By appearing indifferent to their parents, they attempt to create a sense of unimportance in their parents, which is a role they prefer their parents to play rather than feel it themselves.

Similarly, an adolescent's self-esteem is extremely fragile, and teenagers often attack their parents' self-esteem and question their values. Frequently they feel threatened, so they behave in threatening ways. Although they are masters of denial, adolescents know they need their parents' help. Thus, an adolescent's deeper intelligence will always give her parents clues in order to help them see past her overt reluctance for parental input. Parents must remember, the mind wants the best for itself, and deep down teenagers are no different from anyone else. Somewhere in their minds they are inclined to listen to their parents because they need the insight and stability they have to offer.

Another common behavior among adolescents is their attempt to hide their fear of independence and of separating from their parents. Often teenagers are terrified of leaving their family, and thus they need to remain somewhat a child; yet they feel they must fight against these feelings by appearing super-independent.

Many times teens need to know who they really are and where their boundaries are. So they secretly ask you to show them, ask you to say "no" to them so that they will know where to stop—to be able to say "no" to their peers and mean it.

Of all the times it is necessary to understand the value of containment, of building stability into someone simply by being there consistently, it is with adolescents. This comes into play particularly when an argument surfaces or threatens to surface. Here parents can profit immensely from an appreciation of what a therapist does. Good therapists never argue with their patients. They certainly differ with them or, more accurately, have the job of showing them where they differ with themselves. And, of course, parents cannot be as verbally self-contained as therapists. But parents can greatly profit from understanding how important controlling themselves and not firing back are. With a new appreciation of containment, parents will reap all sorts of good consequences.

One other aspect of arguments is helpful to understand. Most of the time what we argue about is not the main issue. And arguments with our teens especially are frequently left-brain communications designed to hide important right-brain issues. For example, a teenager may argue with his parents over what time he has to come home at night. In the process he may give all sorts of reasons why he should be allowed to stay out later. Yet deep down the adolescent is desperately seeking a boundary and is embarrassed about this need. (Of course, when parents are being overly restrictive, adolescents will rightfully complain. To understand whether the primary need of the moment is to loosen the boundaries or to hold to the boundaries is the art of parenting. Learning to listen for the deeper intelligence can help serve as a guide in addressing this ever-present dilemma.) It is important for parents to realize just how much they will be tested during their child's adolescence. Much of the time an adolescent feels chaotic and confused, as if he is coming apart. Anger is therefore a natural by-product of the turmoil teenagers experience. Deep down their anger is a confession of how frustrated they are over their uncertainty. It is also a request to their parents, in effect saying, "Show me how to handle the pressures of life, like the pressures I am putting on you now." An awareness of this process can help any parent be more confident and be of more benefit to the teenager.

One final need of all children, including teenagers, is affirmation, or what is clinically known as *validation*.

Validation is a deep-seated conviction that conveys to the child or adolescent that beyond all the turbulence of daily life we have the abiding belief that the child is okay. It embodies a high form of *commitment,* one of the three core values we all live by. For someone to believe in another person is the deepest form of love. The well-known biblical passage about love affirms this: "[Love] bears all things, *believes* all things, hopes all things, endures all things. Love never fails" (1 Cor. 13:7–8 NKJV, emphasis mine). And it is certainly important for us to verbally say "I love you" from time to time to the teenager we are affirming.

Parents also get a chance indirectly to affirm their kids every day by providing stability, by properly "holding" their kids with the right environment. A large part of this type of affirmation is accomplished when parents just control their tongues. By providing kids the basic stability they need, a parent sends the message, "I believe in you enough to meet your most basic needs for security."

Woody Allen's famous line, "Eighty percent of success is just showing up," certainly relates here. A large percentage of being a good parent is just providing the stability and the containment kids need.

KIDS AND BOUNDARIES

Like every other human being, deep down our kids are afraid of boundaries. Just like us, the life-giving boundaries they need they also fear, because boundaries are also associated with potential pain—abandonment, ridicule, and abuse. Deep down kids have a deeper intelligence just as perceptive as any adult's. They intuitively understand intimacy anxiety, as evidenced by the pain they feel separating from their parents and having to face an adult world. Much of adolescent misbehavior is secretly related to this fear, which explains why adolescents on the one hand have powerful urges to avoid boundaries, to avoid rules—because rules mean real relationships.

Like every other human being, deep down our kids are afraid of boundaries.

The best way of undercutting this fear of boundaries (at the heart of security anxiety) is for parents themselves to overcome it. As a couple stays committed to their marriage, they deliver a powerful message to their son or daughter that says: "See it is okay to live within the boundaries of real commitment. It is safe. You will not be destroyed if you do it yourself."

The best way of undercutting this fear of boundaries (at the heart of security anxiety) is for parents themselves to overcome it.

Kids share with adults the deep-seated belief that one-to-ones are so powerful that they are dangerous. From a very early age, probably even while in their mother's womb, kids are aware of the powerful feelings that one-to-ones evoke. For example, kids are acutely sensitive to being abandoned throughout their development. They also are aware of other powerful emotions associated with one-to-ones, such as during adolescence (and earlier) when both parents and teenagers want to destroy each other—

no matter how much they love each other. In truth, the very love itself at times intensifies anger. The vulnerability adolescents feel over needing their parents and being forced to be separate from them (by simply getting older) prompts tremendous anger.

A few kids hide it, but most adolescents express it through sullenness (although occasionally this confusion erupts into overt hostility). Of course virtually all kids hide from themselves the real reasons for their chronic irritation. They are so passionate about their wish for independence and simultaneously their fear of being independent (their vulnerability) that at the time they overtly experience hate for their parents. Parents, by being human beings, often respond to hatred and seeming ingratitude with normal feelings of hurt and anger. Thus at difficult moments during adolescence (and early childhood, too), both parents and adolescents have been tremendously hurt by the other and have thoughts of destruction. The more someone can hurt you, the greater the potential for anger.

Love and hate or anger often go together, for we are most vulnerable to those we love. The important thing about successfully facing the intensity stirred up in family members during adolescence is to make sure that guilt doesn't rule our lives and thus lead to self-punishing tendencies. Too often, because anger toward someone we love is such an unacceptable idea, we are unaware that guilt is building and deep down we secretly are punishing ourselves. One of the most common ways of achieving self-punishment (designed to alleviate our guilt) is to perpetuate an argument with an adolescent, which almost always is destructive to both parties involved and creates further distance.

Remember, anytime an argument is taking place, *you* can stop it. It takes two to argue. One of the great responses a parent can make when a child is being inappropriately hostile is to contain it, rather than to immediately retaliate with an accusation or to punish the adolescent. Then the adolescent is allowed to experience his own aggression in the face of a controlled person. By containing an outburst and walking away, a parent is building a number of healthy traits into the adolescent. An adolescent has learned that his anger didn't destroy someone, and he has just witnessed a better way to handle powerful emotions by containing and expressing them appropriately.

After an argument with an adolescent, if a parent doesn't become sullen or resentful toward the adolescent, the two powerful messages of love—forgiveness and reconciliation—are sent. I am not suggesting that parents become a doormat or not insist on respect from their teenager; but it is also a fact of life that kids need to feel their relationship with their parent is strong enough to handle their anger. It's better for a parent to teach a child how to express his anger than for him to learn it from someone else.

INTERPRETING LIFE

Sometimes what children need most is a direct interpretation of life—that is, plain old understanding. They need their parents to tell them what is going on. This may mean, for example, explaining why certain rules are enforced. But at other key moments, your youngster may need to present her own ideas and hidden, right-brain understanding on a subject. In this case, you as a parent need to show your deeper awareness to her.

For example, if your teenager makes several passing comments about the homeless or starving people during a time when she is stressed by the fact that she is leaving home (as reflected in her irritable behavior), you could link the two subjects together for her. In effect she is suggesting a link between the ideas of a lack of security (the homeless) and a lack of nurturing (starvation) to her leaving home, which then explains her behavior. Then you might say something like this, "I know you have been worried lately. But I want you to consider something else. Let me ask, do you think your anger lately is prompted by a sense of your losing something here—your stability and the love we have for you—with your moving out being right around the corner? Well, it's normal for you to feel stress about what you're going through in your life right now. And remember, even after you've moved out, your room will still be your room."

THE DEEPER INTELLIGENCE IN YOUNGER CHILDREN

Many times adolescents give us a large picture of what has actually been going on inside of them in a smaller way throughout childhood. Younger children have the same basic needs as adolescents, and adolescent behavior in part can be determined by what has been built into them in their earlier years. Younger children also have two levels of their mind and have a perceptive deeper intelligence that picks up on messages addressed to both the conscious and subconscious levels. Their deeper intelligence is constantly monitoring what their parents do and say, because parents are the primary building blocks in their lives.

This of course means children have the same needs as adolescents for clear boundaries, both physically (their own room or space within a room) and emotionally. Their emotional boundaries can be respectful or disrespectful in a hundred different ways—most commonly by not listening to them and giving their opinion real weight or real consideration at certain moments.

Young children have the same needs as teenagers for

validation of their personhood, containing of their emotional outbursts, and at times an interpretation of what they are going through. At moments, the deeper intelligence will clearly manifest itself through the stories a child tells, as we saw earlier (see page 84) with the young child Elizabeth who was reacting with great alarm to the impending birth of her new sibling. Throughout childhood, again one of the central tasks of parents is to teach (by modeling) their children how to manage turmoil. At moments a child's outburst will be a request to the parents, saying, "Show me how I can keep from being overwhelmed by this situation." When in the face of turmoil, a parent can respond with some equanimity, that sends the child a powerful message of hope.

Children have incredible needs for commitment and stability—a safe environment in which they are free to express themselves. They also ask that others tell them the truth in order to grasp reality and what it is they are becoming (since they incorporate those around them, inconsistencies and all). We have long known about these basic needs children have; the deeper intelligence only shows us how great the needs are and how easy it is to compromise our roles as parents.

THERE ARE NO PERFECT PARENTS

No matter how strongly you desire to be a perfect parent, you will never be one—never. In fact, you will never even be *close* to being a perfect parent! Thus how you manage your failures as a parent is crucial. A genuine apology in the face of a clear error and then resuming a normal life without resorting to ongoing self-criticism is, of course, an ideal way for you to manage failure. In contrast, any ongoing harping or bickering will contain a hidden message, "I want to keep abusing you and in turn I want you to keep abusing me."

We have a lot to learn about how to be better parents. As we become better listeners, particularly for the deeper intelligence and its principles, we will become more capable parents.

CHAPTER ELEVEN

The Deeper Intelligence and Codependency

Codependency has become one of the folk psychology bywords in recent years, but it is a very real phenomenon. What exactly is codependency, and what prompts it? The deeper intelligence shows us it may not exactly be what we've thought. This therapy session provides an example.

The tall, lanky man leaned back in his chair as he talked casually. His therapist, Dr. Adams, said to himself, *He doesn't seem to have a care in the world—but appearances are deceiving.*

Daniel had come to Dr. Adams to learn how to cope with his "wife's problems." As Daniel told it, his wife had developed a drinking problem in the last few years and had progressively gotten more out of control, having several extramarital affairs. Daniel had been crushed by this, but he still loved his wife and wanted to preserve the marriage. Finally, however, the circumstances had gotten to him. He felt overwhelmed and depressed.

He told Dr. Adams, "I've been reading a lot on codependent behavior to try to understand my wife. And I've been learning a lot about our relationship. I was talking to a friend about my therapy, and he suggested I get into group therapy. He knew about a group run by a therapist who is an expert on codependency. I think maybe he's right. He said everyone loves this therapist, he's so good.

"You know, Dr. Adams, I have always had difficulty with you sitting back and just listening. You've explained this to me, and sometimes it makes sense. But at times you seem harsh, and I think sometimes it's cruel not to lead me a little more. You know how uncomfortable I get here at times, particularly with periods of silence. I don't think I could treat people that way. That's why I've thought about group therapy. There would be a lot of feedback."

Dr. Adams knew Daniel had struggled with his therapy for the few months he had been in it. And despite Daniel's discomfort with the process, the doctor knew it was best for the patient to continue talking on his own. Now a thought crossed Dr. Adam's mind: *Hopefully, Daniel's deeper intelligence will tell me why he really wants to leave therapy before he just quits.*

Daniel continued, "We're having a family reunion in two weeks, and I never miss it. I always go back to the small town where my father grew up. I used to stay there with my grandfather in the summers. My grandfather and I were very close. It really upset me when he suddenly died. I was twelve at the time. I still use his old key chain, and on the walls in my study I have two pictures he had in his home. I look at them every day. It's as if a part of him is always with me."

Then Daniel seemed to shift topics. "We've been going to a number of parties, and it's hard for my wife not to drink. My company has had too many parties lately, almost as many as all those committee meetings we've been having, where nothing really gets accomplished. Also, my boss is having trouble with two of my coworkers, and he just won't confront them privately, one-on-one. He needs to do that, though, because that's the only real way to solve the problems."

He then spoke of the bad influence his daughter's friends were having on her: "Our daughter, Jennifer, wanted to drop out of high school and get her G.E.D. at the local junior college, as a number of her friends are doing. I told her she couldn't drop out of school just to be with those lousy friends of hers."

Had Daniel's deeper intelligence cast any new light on the session? Was his deeper mind offering him any wisdom for living out his life? Indeed, it was clearly telling him and his therapist what he truly thought of the idea of group therapy.

By talking about several negative situations concerning groups, Daniel's deeper intelligence was advising him against changing to group therapy. And by telling the story about how his boss needed to deal with some problems one-on-one, it also was recommending Daniel confront his problems in a one-to-one relationship. Furthermore, Daniel's deeper intelligence revealed why he secretly preferred the group: It would help him to continue avoiding the painful experience of separation and loss of his grandfather, with which he had never effectively dealt. Deep down Daniel was convinced that if he ever allowed a true one-to-one relationship to develop, he would be hurt and abandoned, as when he had lost his grandfather.

After reviewing these observations, Dr. Adams further pointed out to Daniel his pattern of avoiding individuality through group experiences and by losing himself in another person (such as wanting Dr. Adams to advise him). Daniel said he didn't completely understand what Dr. Adams was saying. But he then revealed two other painful losses in close relationships he had never mentioned. This was his way of telling Dr. Adams that, yes, his fear of abandonment was behind his avoidance of a true, intimate, one-to-one relationship.

This session was filled with codependent patterns of relating, many of which were quite subtle. In many ways Daniel used them to avoid a true one-to-one. Quietly

187

bringing a friend into therapy by discussing therapy with him; reading a book on codependency; wanting to join a group; wanting advice from a therapist (versus true understanding)—all were subtle ways Daniel tried to change the boundaries of therapy and escape his own individuality. They all involved depending on someone or something other than himself (and his brilliant deeper intelligence).

But isn't a patient involved in an in-depth psychotherapy by definition depending on a therapist? Not in the same sense as a codependent relationship. The only appropriate dependency any patient wants deep down is for a therapist to provide a safe, controlled environment which allows him to express the wisdom of his deeper intelligence. At the appropriate moment, the patient expects his therapist to decode his deeper intelligence, which the therapist has encouraged and allowed him to express. Anything beyond this is inappropriate dependency, and at that moment the therapist demonstrates codependency.

At the very moment Daniel's left brain was proclaiming his freedom from codependency (he had read a book on it and implied that now he understood it), his right brain was revealing how he was a living, breathing, shining example of codependency.

The human mind is fascinating in the ways it can easily fool itself. At the very moment Daniel's left brain was proclaiming his freedom from codependency (he had read a book on it and implied that now he understood it), his right brain was revealing how he was a living, breathing, shining example of codependency.

Without a doubt, this same tendency would have come into play with his wife, which meant that when she drank, she not only would have been expressing her own addictive tendencies, but Daniel's as well.

Daniel shows us that there are many forms of addiction. He was addicted to certain types of dependent relationships.

Not only can we hide dependency in others, we can hide other emotions. Daniel attempted to hide aggressiveness and harshness in Dr. Adams for not guiding him more. If, indeed, Dr. Adams had resorted to guiding Daniel, he would have been cruel at the very moment he took over Daniel's responsibility for his own life, which then would have made Dr. Adams guilty or "bad" for his failure as a therapist, in addition to being aggressive. Secretly, Daniel wanted Dr. Adams to be the cruel one so he himself would be free of such a painful emotional state. Certainly, by subtly enabling his wife to be out of control, Daniel was encouraging her aggressiveness (cruelty to the family and others through her drinking), as well as her "badness," her failure.

Because of the remarkable ability of the human mind to disguise its motives, it is possible to hide any emotion in others. If we are going to truly understand codependency and all that it has to teach us, we must understand our minds are capable of encouraging co-anything—co-anger, co-guilt (co-badness), co-sexuality, co-unfaithfulness.

The deeper intelligence significantly broadens our understanding of codependency, clarifying how subtle it can be. Below Daniel's charming and laid-back demeanor lurked powerful emotions, just as they do in all of us, no matter what face we show to the world.

WHEN SHOULD WE SEEK ADVICE?

To the right brain, because of its need for wholeness and independence, advice is often experienced as aggressive, indulgent, and overgratifying. It is amazing that such a simple and well-intended action as giving advice can have such unfortunate meanings, but nevertheless it is true. To give advice in therapy is, deep down, to both take over for someone at the precise moment he is trying to learn independence (one of his three great needs), which is to overgratify him, and to keep him from making his own decision. This is particularly true in light of the fact he possesses a brilliant deeper intelligence that his true self yearns to express.

To the right brain, because of its need for wholeness and independence, advice is often experienced as aggressive, indulgent, and overgratifying.

This is particularly true if a person is depending on others too much and holding himself back. There are many situations where we should make a decision on our own. There is also a time to get counseling—the biblical proverb advises, "Without counsel, plans go awry / But in the multitude of counselors they are established" (Prov. 15:22 NKJV). But after getting input from others, the decision must be our own.

There are plenty of times and places for one person to counsel another, but one place that is not true is in psychotherapy. (Actually therapy involves a number of coun-

190

selors. One is the therapist who advises his patient to listen to his deeper intelligence. A number of other experienced therapists also are on record as counselling a patient to do the same. The patient's own deeper intelligence serves as another counselor, if the patient will allow it to be heard. The consensual wisdom from all these sources is for a patient to let his capable deeper intelligence lead the way in therapy—to live by the laws of the deeper mind.) A person enters therapy to obtain wholeness and to find out what his deeper intelligence knows. That is why there is a big difference in therapists who primarily counsel and those who listen to a person's deeper mind. Thus, advice is an aggressive intrusion whereby a therapist fails to model self-control. The bottom line is that advice-giving on the part of a therapist is secretly codependent behavior—because it encourages dependence.

Obviously, advice-giving in everyday life may also have similar negative ramifications, and we should not advise others as often as we think we should. It is too easy to get "addicted" to others taking over for us, to have our true identity undermined. The fear of being an individual is the greatest fear we have. Ironically being independent is one of our greatest needs.

SECOND EFFECTS

A helpful way to evaluate different relationships as to whether or not codependent tendencies are present, is to look at what I call "second effects," or hidden effects to actions or words. For example, if Daniel had thought through the potential hidden effects of group therapy in light of his three basic needs of autonomy, integrity, and commitment (in particular), he could have recognized many tendencies toward codependency in his behavior.

If prior to therapy Daniel had had some meaningful understanding of his three deepest needs, he would have

191

immediately recognized that group therapy was a compromise in all three areas. This is primarily because group therapy could not offer him his own unique space but shared space (decreased commitment), it could not honor much of his autonomy (because others would do the work for him and allow him to hide), and because it could not offer him a whole or completely private environment (integrity). While group therapy claimed to be therapy, at many moments it was the opposite of therapy since it helped people to hide from themselves.

It is true that people have to learn to function in groups. But even within larger nurturing families, I have seen many persons who never found their individuality. The more complete we are as individuals, the better group members we will be. Our first task in life is to become a true individual—to honor the individuality we have been given.

Of course codependent issues and the second effects that inevitably arise are not limited to close relationships like marriage. As you read the following incident, which occurred in a work environment, try to pick up "hidden effects" in Randolph's behavior.

BOARDROOM BATTLEGROUND

As Barry slid into his chair in the corporate boardroom, he couldn't help but wonder exactly why Randolph, his senior vice-president, had wanted him to attend. It wasn't all that unusual for the different department heads to bring one of their top assistants to an important meeting. But Barry had noticed a pattern: Whenever there was a meeting that promised a major conflict with another department, then Randolph seemed to really want his help. Barry actually enjoyed the give and take of the boardroom; it reminded him of an athletic contest. But it seemed Randolph was uncomfortable in these sorts of situations.

Just as Barry sat down, he heard Randolph chatting lightly with another senior vice-president, asking him if he had heard about the crazy situation in their advertising firm. Randolph said, "The president, Bill Jemison, lost control of himself after a meeting and he actually punched his partner, Drew, nearly knocking him out. Now Drew is leaving and planning on suing him."

Barry's ears picked up and the thought ran through his mind, *I wonder if that's what Randolph's afraid of here—somebody getting out of control in our meeting?*

Randolph casually went on, "I had a brother who was like that. If he disagreed with you, he would fight you at the drop of a hat." Randolph chuckled as he told that story, but Barry wondered if he was really chuckling deep down. Now a few things made more sense. Randolph was always referring to Barry as a former Marine—"My favorite Marine"—which, indeed, he had been.

Barry remembered the many times Randolph was about to cave in to demands from other departments and not protect the people under him. If Barry hadn't fought to get Randolph to stand up for his department, unnecessary and unwise changes would have occurred. Randolph was persuasive once he made up his mind, but frequently he waffled on a decision, particularly when there was conflict.

Now Barry had some awareness of why Randolph was the way he was, and the insight had come in Randolph's own words. At the exact moment he was experiencing the pressures of an impending conflict, Randolph had talked about people losing control and assaulting others or being assaulted. Barry thought again to himself, *I'll bet that's why Randolph's indecisive; he's afraid of being hurt or losing control and hurting somebody.* And Barry was right.

In some ways Randolph recognized that he was not as tough as Barry, and at times he clearly depended on Barry's tenacity and strength. "Half-brilliantly," Randolph compensated for his weakness by selecting someone who was strong where he was weak. Nevertheless, he was

193

paying a price in his own personality and individuality for letting Barry do what ideally he should have been able to handle himself.

Certainly, teamwork is important in that we all have different gifts. There will always be times we have to accept our limitations. However, Randolph's problem with decision making and not standing on his own was that it was excessive—too much dependence, which meant that it presented him with problems in other areas of his life, too.

Through a better understanding of our real nature, we will become more sensitive to our individuality and that of others. And when we do, we will less frequently attempt to take over for others, be less inclined to tell them what to do, and perhaps better learn how to motivate others by honoring their individual abilities. It will make us better parents, better spouses, better friends, and better bosses.

Yet indecisiveness and similar retreats from individuality take place all the time in relationships. One of the most common forms we see is the failure to take responsibility. Many, if not most of us, struggle with this issue. Yet, when we don't admit our faults, we miss out on one of the greatest attributes we can have—courage. And courage is another mark of a true individual.

Make no mistake—becoming a true individual, becoming the unique person of character we can be, is incredibly hard. The essence of a famous proverb is if you can control yourself, you are greater than someone who rules a city.[1] In other words, when you can master your individuality, you are accomplishing one of the most difficult tasks in the world. Yet our individuality is our greatest gift. It is who we are.

The deeper intelligence holds out to us the potential awareness that we are prone to denying our individuality much more often than we think. In situation after situation, the deeper intelligence attempts to help us see who we are and the individual we can become. It is acutely

194

aware that the phenomenon of codependency is much larger than we think it is and that codependency wears a thousand disguises. If we hear the voice of the deeper intelligence, we can begin to rise to the greatest challenge we can have: to be ourselves.

You may be uncomfortable with my talk about individuality, i.e., is it somewhat synonymous with self-centeredness? True, we must not allow selfishness to lead us away from the important notion of community. One of the most important tasks in life is to learn to live unselfishly in community.

Yet our individuality, when properly understood, leads us toward community and not away from it.

Yet our individuality, when properly understood, leads us *toward* community and not away from it. Individuals who truly face who they are don't get caught up in codependent traps of blaming others or encouraging others to secretly express certain roles for them. Real individuals don't use other people, they love them. Individuals understand the basic code of life—autonomy, commitment, and integrity—and thus can appreciate what it truly means "to love your neighbor as yourself," because they know who they are and who their neighbor is. Real individuals appreciate other individuals. They recognize the value of individuals—how capable individuals are and how much individuals have to teach other individuals. In the end true individuals make the best and most unselfish community members.

A NEW UNDERSTANDING OF CODEPENDENCY

As we have looked at codependency, the deeper intelligence has once again revealed more clearly who we are. We have seen how subtle codependency can be, how often people think they have conquered it only to have secretly adopted another codependent way of relating. Beyond identifying this behavior, the deeper intelligence over and over has pinpointed the primary motivation behind it: Fear.

We have seen how subtle codependency can be, how often people think they have conquered it only to have secretly adopted another codependent way of relating.

What has been missing in our understanding of codependency (prior to the breakthrough to the deeper intelligence) is the failure to appreciate the primary cause behind this unhealthy behavior. For example, a person may see codependency as rescuing others, being overly protective, failing to confront others, being overly conscientious/perfectionistic, being a workaholic, being indecisive, and being excessively submissive. Only when we begin to see that the primary function of all of these behaviors is to prevent true individuality and thus prevent development of a true one-to-one will we gain mastery over them.

Overlooking this basic issue had led to codependent

behaviors simply changing forms and continuing in disguised ways. For example, a former codependent "rescuer" can become withdrawn, critical (labeling his mate as dysfunctional and bad), or substitute another way of losing his identity. He may stop covering up for a spouse that drinks but then might allow the mate to make all the important decisions. Whichever role is assumed, the outcome is the same: True individuality and true intimacy are discouraged.

The deeper intelligence teaches us how easy it is to perpetuate codependent patterns. Until the individual understands the reason behind his behavior, he will almost certainly repeat the codependent behavior in different forms. When friends understand these issues they can model healthier behavior in helping others overcome disguised codependency. By knowing the basic rules of life, friends can know when to confront and point out (interpret) a pattern of codependency rather than playing into it.

The deeper intelligence has taken us deep into our hearts and revealed a basic inclination we all have at moments, far more pervasive than we ever realized, to deny ourselves the very individuality we long to express.

CHAPTER TWELVE

The Deeper Intelligence and Therapy

*"The truth must dazzle gradually or every
man be blind."*
Emily Dickinson

The doors on the car wouldn't stay on, particularly the back doors. Over and over the woman tried to install the doors. At times, however, another new door would show up beside her in a heap of different size doors. Other times she would walk across a parking lot or a field and find herself carrying a door, then try to fit it on the left side of the car. From time to time an intruder would come through the back door while she was attaching a door and interrupt her, then slide out the other side of the car. Over and over the woman played with the doors to no avail.

This imagery kept running through Meg's mind, alternating with a mild restlessness and agitation. She would rouse slightly in her sleep and then fall back into her dream, hoping this time she would solve the puzzle. Finally she could escape into sleep no longer, and she simply lay there in her bed, her mind racing and her troubles growing by the minute.

It was 5:30 in the morning, and Meg had been up once during the night with her fourteen-month-old daughter, Millie, who had slept for a grand total of three and a half hours. Staring Meg in the face was one more day in a string of long, exhausting days that seemed to her would never end. Meg was depressed.

An anti-depressant from her family doctor had helped some, but she was still not her old self. *Maybe,* she thought to herself, *it's just stress—my new baby, a job I don't want to go to, and just having moved.*

Fed up with feeling overwhelmed, Meg reluctantly sought help from a psychiatrist, Dr. Ron Baker. Before this step she had tried everything: trying to understand herself, reading self-help books, talking with friends and a counselor at church, and finally taking medication. Nothing had really helped.

Like so many others, Meg had viewed seeking help from a therapist as a last resort. Now, sitting in his office, Meg unfolded her story freely. She mentioned that she had almost canceled her appointment, and she wondered aloud why she might be depressed. "I have had a lot of changes in the last year—a new baby, we sold our house, and I had to keep working, which I resent in a way."

As Meg elaborated on the details for several minutes, Dr. Baker waited patiently. He thought, *She's talking about a lot of changes and dropping a few hints. But so far she hasn't told me what the real issues are. There's something more powerful going on.*

Meg went on: "And the wreck, I almost forgot to mention that. Last month my station wagon was totaled, and I was trapped in the car for forty-five minutes, scared to death. I wasn't really hurt, just scared."

Now you're getting closer, Dr. Baker thought.

Later Meg mentioned the death of a grandfather in the last year, and a close friend had been paralyzed in an accident.

At that point Dr. Baker showed Meg her train of thought: car wreck, being trapped, a friend being injured, being tied down by a new baby and a job, losing someone she was close to. Dr. Baker gently showed her how these issues were so much on her mind, they even played themselves out when she was in any enclosed, private relationship, such as the one in therapy with him. Meg hadn't wanted to come to therapy, which meant that deep down some notion was controlling her. Whenever she found herself in a definite relationship, she felt entrapped and that she would be either hurt directly or hurt by someone's leaving.

With that insight now somewhat more apparent to Meg, even more thoughts of painful relationships came pouring out as her deeper intelligence led the way. She had had a terrible delivery, twenty-six hours long, and nearly lost her baby. Just after Millie was born, Meg had contracted phlebitis and was in bed for nearly three weeks. And the recent death of her grandfather had reminded Meg of the sudden death of her favorite uncle, to whom she had been quite close, when she was just fourteen.

Dr. Baker realized how striking the patterns to her thinking were. The ideas that controlled Meg clearly told her danger was just around the next corner, as it had been before. Now Dr. Baker once more pointed out the familiar pattern: Meg linked closeness with being entrapped and hurt. He showed her how this also was being played out in therapy; she very subtly wanted to escape the one-to-one there by wanting to cancel her appointment.

Meg's deeper intelligence rewarded Dr. Baker's helpful perspective by ending on two important notes. First, she mentioned how well her husband was doing in his job and that soon she might not have to work and would be able to stay home with her daughter. In essence, she was saying, "Dr. Baker, you're doing a good job. You are lightening my load already."

Second, Meg mentioned an affair she had almost had since returning to work, something which had significantly disturbed her and caused her much suffering. Dr. Baker ended the session by telling her, "You're telling us that all this pressure of living with the sense of being trapped in relationships has caused you to have the urge to step outside of your marriage."

Over the next several months Meg improved dramatically, although her therapy was characterized by familiar struggles. Time after time she presented disguised ideas of people being entrapped and endangered, and then she would mention stopping therapy or cutting back. All of these were reflections of how her fears came alive in her therapy. Each time they revealed the secret fear that drove her life. But with Dr. Baker's help, Meg was able to stay in therapy, and new insights occurred. During one session, she was able to understand one of several nightmares she'd been having.

Eventually, Meg saw many self-defeating ways that she had avoided many commitments in her daily life. She had dropped out of graduate school, and she often broke promises made to friends. Slowly, she came to terms with her fears, and as she did her life improved. Her confidence grew, her decisions were better, and her depression went away.

WHAT CAN THERAPY ACCOMPLISH?

What did psychotherapy actually do for Meg? Why was she better?

Meg had come to psychotherapy with a very specific question: Why am I depressed? And now, because of the environment Dr. Baker created, as well as his giving Meg's deeper intelligence an opportunity to express itself, Meg had gotten some clear-cut answers. Prior to therapy, Meg had come up with a few answers on her own, but she couldn't take them far enough to make any lasting headway. With therapy giving her someone to react to, however, her deeper intelligence was able to take her much further into understanding why she was blocked and depressed.

In essence, to see how Meg would react Dr. Baker had set up a human relationship laboratory of the most powerful kind—an intimate, one-to-one. This laboratory experience was exactly what she needed. By looking at her fears face-to-face and eventually seeing that they were not true in her relationship with Dr. Baker, Meg was able to see how she overreacted with distrust (often resulting in avoidance) in other enclosed situations. *The truth had set Meg free.*

Patients use the powerful one-to-one with their therapist to work through fear and to find a healthy person to build wholeness into them and repair their deficits.

Much too often, however, therapists don't see how their patients are reacting to them—how the deeper intelligence is using the relationship with the therapist as a practical laboratory experience. At the heart of therapy the patient is *always reacting* to the therapist in a central way. I am not talking only about transference (see discussion that follows), in which the patient distorts who the therapist is, but about how the patient reacts to a therapist and whether he meets the patient's three basic needs. A patiently constantly looks to a therapist to create as strong an environment as possible and thereby build wholeness into him. Therapists never realized the extent of the power they had moment by moment for building strength in their patients until the deeper intelligence revealed it.

Here we have arrived at a crucial point in understanding how our minds operate. We tend to link—associate—familiar situations in our mind far more often and to a much greater degree than we realize. The mind works by way of reminders or triggers. It is this capacity for linking, for association, which gives therapy much of its power (and its pain).

In the one-to-one of therapy, the patient is immediately reminded of other important one-to-one relationships, particularly ones where she has been hurt. This allows for a healing of the mind to take place, because embedded, frightening ideas can surface and be conquered. The primary fixed idea in the back of everyone's mind, which tends to rule our lives, is that private one-to-one relationships are dangerous "because that is where I got hurt before." The deeper intelligence masterfully shows the therapist this fixed idea.

Other related, common fixed ideas which have to be dealt with include:

1. "I am afraid that if I allow a true one-to-one to develop, I will be abandoned."
2. "Close relationships remind me of that terrible realization that one day I will die."
3. "I must also avoid close relationships, because I am afraid I will hurt someone else with my anger (or by leaving them)."
4. "I must avoid definite situations in general because they remind me of being closed in. I never like to be closed in in any way."
5. "I deserve to be punished because somebody really hurt me—punished me—in an important one-to-one, and I must have deserved it. Sometimes I get so angry I want to punish myself. It is my role at times to be punished. Therefore I will seek out relationships which cause me to suffer at times."
6. "I must settle for compromises in one-to-one relationships. I want closeness but I fear it. I want to be loved but I also need to be punished. Therefore, I must choose people who appear to be consistent but really can't be. I must choose people who appear to love me but will also punish me."

So there are two important aspects to therapy: First, stability: an environment which repairs defects in a patient's personality because it offers wholeness. Secondly, understanding: an environment which causes the fear which controls the patient's life to surface. This is where the important concept known as transference comes into play.

Transference occurs because the mind works by way of reminders or triggers. The brilliantly perceptive deeper intelligence constantly reads each environment we find ourselves in for its basic qualities. Is it open and therefore nonthreatening, or enclosed and potentially dangerous? Is it like an anxiety-producing ride on an airplane or like a free and easy Sunday afternoon in the park with friends? After assessing each new situation, the mind reacts to the environment depending on previous experiences in similar environments. This comparing of environments goes on all of the time, and this is what creates the phenomenon known as transference.

In Meg's situation, she reacted to Dr. Baker as though she were in a relationship or enclosed situation which meant loss (grandfather, friend, baby, or her own life) or a dangerous entrapment (a car wreck, a prolonged labor and delivery). To again have a full life, Meg had to realize how her mind was overreacting and reading danger into healthy, enclosed relationships or situations.

Transference is an important idea but there is one major problem with it. Therapists who don't know how to listen to the deeper intelligence use the concept of transference to explain away their own errors. The deeper intelligence reveals that many times a therapist attributes a lack of progress in therapy to a patient's "transference problem" when, in fact, the therapist himself is the real problem as inadvertently he is failing to meet a patient's basic needs. For example, a therapist might break confidentiality in a "minor way" and speak briefly with a third party about a patient but never make the connection when in the following session the patient has become more depressed and distrustful. The therapist might blame the worsening of symptoms on transference, seeing the problem as a patient needing to work through his tendency to distort reality instead of recognizing that the break in confidentiality was of major importance to the patient's right brain (and led to the symptoms).

Another important aspect of therapy is that it brings a fresh opinion to the problem. Meg's own deeper mind provided the hidden pattern to her thinking that shaped her life, but she herself couldn't see the pattern that was crystal clear to Dr. Baker. A therapist's role is to spot the thought patterns after the patient demonstrates them. The therapist must listen to the patient's ideas, not just to the literal stories or feelings, and consider that every story could apply to the patient himself or to the therapist.

Too often therapists fail because they are left-brain-oriented and thus fail to deal with the right brain.

Too often therapists fail because they are left-brain-oriented and thus fail to deal with the right brain. Whatever the path of healing therapists and patients choose, however, one thing is certain: We now have some clear-cut answers as to how psychotherapy works and doesn't work. Growth in understanding ourselves ultimately comes with a high price tag—discomfort. We must give up our old, comfortable ways of seeing ourselves. One of the central aspects of therapy, in fact, is facing the discomfort we have blocked out. Wholeness comes only when we bring our left and right brains together. We must remember that our right brain or unconscious mind not only protects us by blocking out painful thoughts, but also through the deeper intelligence it helps us face the pain in doses we can tolerate. Because we all have a fear of intimate relationships, this means that, at some point, every patient who is given an opportunity to utilize the deeper intelligence in therapy will come to fear her therapist.

WHY ARE WE SO AFRAID OF ENCLOSED SITUATIONS?

The question which is so puzzling is why the part of our deeper mind I have labeled the punishing intelligence is so sensitive to enclosed situations. Why is this fear so universal and prominent in everyone, even those who don't recall being traumatized earlier in their lives?

One answer, of course, is that many more of us have been traumatized than we realize. Numerous times I have seen a patient continually talk about dangerous relationships and eventually observe their deeper intelligence uncover a powerful, traumatic event they had forgotten about. Also, it is quite clear the one-to-one in therapy (as in all other intimate one-to-ones) reminds us of a future trauma: the death of those we love and our own eventual demise. This fear will show up time and again. You must work it through, or it will lead you to bad decisions. Beyond what has been discussed, the deeper intelligence does not give us exact reasons for this deep-going hypersensitivity to intimate relationships—what I have called security anxiety—through it clearly hints at answers I shall show in the next chapter.

Nevertheless, working through this fear is at the heart of therapy, because this is the same fear that so greatly affects our lives and choices in countless ways.

The tendency to run from the discomfort we need to face is so great it has led to several deeply ingrained myths about therapy, such as, pick a therapist with whom you feel comfortable (warm, caring, etc.). In contrast, the deeper intelligence in many ways says the exact opposite—ignore your conscious feelings and pick a therapist who creates an environment that (1) lets you work through your pain and (2) lets you hear the deeper mind's messages. Comfortable therapy can be costly; all the healing that needs to take place doesn't, because the deep-going healing the deeper intelligence recommends is ignored. Meg illustrated this, as she sought out numerous comfortable alternatives or pseudo-therapies (medication, books, advice from friends), all to no avail.

We must learn that in all our relationships there are times not to run from discomfort. Many times discomfort in a marriage, for example, only means there is a challenge to overcome, an issue to work through. Moments of conflict are to be expected, even welcomed.

IS A GOOD FRIEND AS HELPFUL AS A THERAPIST?

Meg's story brings into the forefront the question of whether friends fit into the role of therapist. Not infrequently we hear that friends often can substitute as therapists. In churches we see courses on lay counseling. Even various professionals are fond of quoting "studies" that show the most important attributes for a counselor or therapist are caring and warmth. One well-known therapist even advises in his books that one can use minimally trained lay therapists in place of licensed therapists.[1]

Is there a difference in a friend and a therapist? Don't all the different types of counseling essentially do the same thing? Is there a difference in counseling and psychotherapy? What are the most important attributes for a therapist? Aren't warmth and caring all that really matter in a therapist in the long run?

Once again we turn to the deeper intelligence for answers—clear, unmistakable answers. As we might expect, there's a left-brain answer and a right-brain answer to these questions. And what sometimes passes for left-brain wisdom is right-brain foolishness.

Meg's situation again provides insight. In addition to reading and analyzing herself on her own, Meg had tried talking with friends and had also consulted a pastoral counselor, all to no avail. Each of these approaches would have addressed almost exclusively her left brain, despite the fact that her problem lay in her right brain, where her fears were hidden. While books, friends, and counselors may all in their own way make efforts at looking below the surface—at providing right-brain input—they all would be significantly limited in their ability to hear the right brain. This is because books and friends are usually trying to tell someone something, instead of listening to what the deeper intelligence has to say in a particular situation at a particular moment in time.

While many counselors make sincere efforts to listen, most would be primarily seeking left-brain input because they don't yet know how the right brain works. The language of the right brain I am describing is very new information. Until recently no one had really heard the deeper intelligence speak in its own clear language, nor ever knew it existed.

Meg's experience reveals using friends as therapists or using an advice-giving or counseling sort of approach has very limited effectiveness. Unfortunately her situation is all too common.

Friends cannot be therapists precisely *because* they are friends. Most of the time friends simply can't be objective enough. Friends can bear burdens, share experiences, encourage each other, and laugh and play together. Friends usually spend a lot of time with each other in unstructured settings. A fulfilled oneness is a hallmark of a good friendship. Oneness is indeed a wonderful thing, but therapy has an entirely different task. A therapist is attempting to clarify individuality and a person's problems in order to *build strength* through observing and building strong boundaries. In a friendship, the lack of clear boundaries, the togetherness, stands in the way of the goal, healthy therapy, where by necessity the focus is on the individual.

In each particular role of friend or therapist, a person's greatest strength in one role is the greatest weakness in the other. A friend, for example, offers unity and oneness, but not well-defined individuality and clear, strong boundaries. In therapy, the emphasis is not on unity, but on individuality and distinct boundaries. Of course, it is more fun to be a friend, but there are plenty of times people need discipline, boundaries, and definition—not oneness. (Almost paradoxically, however, the healthier and more complete an individual becomes, often the better friend he's able to be.) The same holds true in parenting. Parents at certain moments must be different toward their children from friends, as they have to set boundaries, discipline, and admonish.

Even friends who understand how the deeper intelligence communicates can't really be therapists, because we can "hide" in our friends and won't clearly be able to see ourselves. We will tend to subconsciously focus more on our friend's problem in a self-protective way in order to take our mind off of our problem. Then we won't really be able to clearly define our problem because we will see it tied up with our friend. The deeper intelligence has taught us this crucial lesson and made clear that the way around this ever-present tendency to hide our pain in someone else is to eliminate the potential for hiding. To clearly see (define) ourselves, we must eliminate the potential for externalizing our problems, which is something a therapist can do far better than a friend. (A friend can share a problem. A therapist can define a problem but can't share it in the same way as a friend. We need both.)

Even friends who understand how the deeper intelligence communicates can't really be therapists.

This is why the anonymity of a therapist is so important because it enables a person to get a clear-cut look at himself, since the therapist keeps himself hidden in the relationship. In essence, the deeper intelligence says to the therapist, "Don't get in the way of the picture I am taking of myself by presenting your issues. I don't need to know anything about you right now. I need a really clear picture of myself to see what I have to overcome."

But don't get me wrong about the value of friendships. While I have stressed the differences between friends and therapists and how on an ongoing basis friends can't be therapists, friendship definitely can be therapeutic.

The better you know yourself, the better friend you can be. Then you can know when to encourage, when to share, and when to stop enabling someone's unhealthy behavior. No one in the world can share a problem in the same way as a friend. A friend can stay with you as long as it's necessary to comfort you—like a good mother who can stay up all night with a sick child. Marriage, for example, is ultimately two good friends standing by each other, sharing each other's burdens, until death parts them. Never underestimate the need for friendship; it is the essence of life.

ADVICE GIVING VERSUS UNDERSTANDING

Advice giving, what we often refer to as counseling, is perhaps the most common way of failing to utilize the brilliant deeper mind. Advice from friends and others can be helpful at times, but certainly in therapy it has very limited value. We have seen time after time that when therapists try to advise or directly confront a patient (as a friend might), the patient casually begins talking about things being out of control and boundaries being violated.

Advice giving, what we often refer to as counseling, is perhaps the most common way of failing to utilize the brilliant deeper mind.

For example, Albert, seemingly a compassionate therapist who believed in being straightforward, told his patient, Megan, that she should confront her boss directly for overworking her and taking advantage of her devotion to her job. Albert encouraged Megan, "Stand up for yourself—nobody else is going to do it." Megan thought Albert's idea was right on target, but almost immediately she mentioned something new about her boss—how he frequently lost his temper and intruded in her job, making decisions he should let her make. Megan's left brain thought Albert was a wonderful therapist, but her right brain thought he was behaving just as her boss did.

Once again we see a therapist who didn't understand one very important factor in the relationship with his patient: the boundary of independence. This is why a therapist can do things a friend can't. A therapist's stockin-trade is his implementation of clear, distinct boundaries. A therapist must understand where the boundaries of commitment, independence (autonomy), and integrity stand. He must understand that the deeper intelligence knows that these boundaries are in different places from where the left brain or conscious mind thinks they are. For example, the left brain may want advice while the deeper intelligence insists on autonomy, because it's better for us in the long run.

The deeper intelligence cries out for a therapist who will let it expose its wisdom and not a therapist who imposes his advice (really his will) on the patient.

While there are certain similarities in good counseling and good psychotherapy, such as listening in a sensitive way, we nevertheless must ask, "Listening to *what?*" The therapist who doesn't listen to the right brain or the deeper intelligence is in reality barely listening, and certainly not listening to the patient's deepest and most powerful motivations.

In today's "information age," we often find ourselves surrounded by advice on television, in books, and from friends. There are a lot of people telling you what to do and offering easy answers. The problem is that easy answers are frequently exactly that—easy. And, usually, the easier something is, the less value it is to us.

Rarely do you hear someone telling you to learn to listen, particularly to learn to listen to yourself.

Rarely do you hear someone telling you to learn to listen, particularly to learn to listen to yourself. It is harder and requires more work than being spoon-fed with advice. In the long run learning to listen—including learning to listen to ourselves—offers better results, because there is a law built into the universe that you reap what you sow.

Frequently I hear references to people wanting practical help. Advice columnists, radio talk-show hosts, and certain counselors often refer to what they are attempting to provide as "practical help," and either directly or indirectly imply that therapies which take time and look deeper aren't terribly practical. The primary idea behind these pop psychology approaches is the "quick fix." Many times these folk will offer testimonials from someone who took their advice, applied it well, and are now fine.

My major problem with this type of approach to problems of the mind is that it just isn't true in the long run. In contrast, the deeper intelligence knows it takes time to bring about a healing, and the most frequent way the right brain itself describes therapy is "going to school." The deeper intelligence consistently compares therapy to a prolonged educational experience. (However, I have seen numerous people benefit from even a brief therapy which utilizes their deeper intelligence. Even when therapy is brief the deeper intelligence offers significant potential for healing.) Whenever a patient wants to leave therapy prematurely, invariably the deeper intelligence will bring up stories about people who shouldn't drop out of college or the like. The deeper intelligence wisely understands that neither Rome nor people are built in a day. Of course, we all know the value of a well-timed suggestion, but suggestions can never take the place of the need for deeper understanding.

WHICH THERAPY IS BEST?

How effective are the other forms of therapy you see

around you—family therapy, couples therapy, group therapy, and different varieties of individual therapy? While some learning and relief can take place in other forms of therapy, the difference between left-brain therapy and right-brain therapy is like daylight and darkness. Remember that the one-to-one relationship is the bedrock of all our relationships. Regardless of how much we may enjoy and gain strength from relationships in groups, the one-to-one relationship is the one that gives us our basic strength and identity. And so it is that the intense, focused one-to-one relationship between patient and therapist offers the most complete healing.

I believe that an individual therapy that is centered on listening to the deeper intelligence offers the best and clearest route to healing. Robert Langs makes this case well in his book *Rating Your Psychotherapist* as he shows that patients have taught us what they really need in therapy.[2] Langs demonstrated that patients themselves teach us what they really need from a therapist and that secretly patients themselves are constantly teaching their therapist.

The technical name for the type of therapy examined in this book is "communicative (or communicative interactional) psychotherapy." It draws its name from the awareness that the patient and therapist are constantly communicating (often secretly)—the patient is always reading the therapist (and vice-versa)—and that this communication / interaction is central to the healing process. The therapist constantly communicates through the environment he creates and by his understanding or lack of understanding of what the patient's deeper intelligence is saying. The patient's deeper intelligence uses the environment that the therapist creates to reveal where the patient's problems are. In other words, therapy is constantly alive moment by moment. This is the beauty of the communicative approach.

As I recommend communicative therapy above other

forms, I do so as someone who has tried and been exposed to many different forms of therapy. At times I have patients who simply will not tolerate listening to their deeper intelligence, who insist on advice-based or less in-depth forms of therapy. In each case, I still listen for the deeper mind and never fail to hear its voice. And whenever possible I always attempt to teach patients that they have a deeper intelligence and that it is trying to lead them in a certain healthy direction. Many times I have to gradually move patients into the environment that they really need. The same is true of therapists new to this approach.

Sometimes working with therapists to whom this approach seems so different, I suggest they select one patient to begin working with in this way. This sort of approach allows a therapist to go at their own pace without feeling greatly pressured. What often happens is that therapists soon discover for themselves that the deeper intelligence is alive, and they begin to look for it. Once this happens, other important changes begin to take care of themselves as these therapists begin to grasp why the deeper intelligence needs to be approached in certain ways. Understanding always helps.

One group of therapists that seem to quickly see the value of listening for the deeper intelligence are graduate students in training just starting to work with patients. Several times I have had young students learning the communicative approach tell me how much an understanding of the deeper intelligence has helped settle them down as therapists. Over and over they tell me how much better it feels not to be totally flying by the seat of their pants.

I do not want to imply that other forms of therapy are without benefit. Many noncommunicative therapists are consciously very sensitive people who provide a safe nurturing environment; who don't overtly criticize their patients; who make sincere efforts to empathize with their patients, relating to them in a warm, kind fashion; who

215

don't retaliate if insulted by a patient; and who make serious attempts to understand their patients on a deeper level. At many points these devoted therapists honor a patient's deeper needs and in so doing are of help to their patients.

The deeper intelligence asks that we become just as sensitive to the right brain as the left and asks that we understand both parts of our mind. We are talking about therapists taking the next step in understanding the mind.

Yet the breakthrough to the mind I am describing asks more of us as therapists than all those well-intended approaches. The deeper intelligence asks that we become just as sensitive to the right brain as the left and asks that we understand both parts of our mind. We are talking about therapists taking the next step in understanding the mind. The deeper intelligence repeatedly shows us better ways of helping people, better ways of discovering and modifying our deepest motivations. The deeper intelligence brings standards of accountability to therapy that we have never had before.

My own pilgrimage as a therapist has been one of being open to learning, to finding out whatever would be most beneficial to my patients. This is also where Robert Langs started. As I have said, at the time he discovered the deeper intelligence, he was supervising a group of individual therapists from a variety of training backgrounds. He expected to find many equally effective forms of therapy.

Instead, in every case he encountered a deeper intelligence that always attempted to steer the therapy in a consistent direction. And the deeper mind was quite definite—and consistent—in speaking about what it needed.

As a student and colleague of Dr. Langs's, I have made similar observations and come to a similar conclusion. My journey through eclecticism ended in my becoming a communicative therapist, after I heard the clear language of the deeper intelligence. As I began to rely on it, I saw that results with my patients were much better than before. Of course, many noncommunicative therapists make similar claims about getting good results, which can make things very confusing for laypeople. Yet that is why I think the discovery of the deeper intelligence is even more important: It can tell us clearly in its own words if we are making real progress or simply continuing to avoid our pain.

I believe that psychotherapy research in the future will validate the findings of communicative therapy. Even now the communicative approach to the mind is the only therapy that seems to meet scientific criteria for validation. (Research in psychotherapy has been difficult and deficient up to this point, due to the lack of a method of validation.)[3]

Obviously, I am making a number of strong statements, all of which have not been completely established scientifically—yet. Because I believe these claims I am making does not make them true—or false. While we must wait for complete scientific validation of what I am proposing, we do have adequate criteria for validating the communicative approach. The deeper intelligence will do one of two things to indicate it has been heard: First it will make a positive statement of some type about something or someone functioning particularly well, as if to say, "Yes doctor, you've heard me, good job." Secondly, it will often reveal new information, such as recalling traumatic events that were behind painful emotional symptoms. When this occurs, it is as if the deeper intelligence is saying, "Yes doctor, you're on target, and here is the reason behind my behavior. I haven't told you or my conscious mind until now."

There is no experience for a therapist quite like having the deeper intelligence validate that you heard it. For example, a patient, Larkin, had to miss a few therapy sessions for unavoidable reasons but had accepted my recommendation that it was best for him to own his space—the appointment time—while he was gone, which meant paying for it. Nevertheless, Larkin came in the following session consciously wondering if therapy was worth the money since he had to miss some. In the same session Larkin talked about how much more nurturing he had become at work and home, how much better his depression was, and then talked about how his whole family had watched a mother bird meticulously build a nest in a tree next to their house. For several weeks his family had watched four little birds grow up and eventually fly off. Larkin was telling himself that therapy was a nest for him where he was in the process of growing and developing. Even while he was away from therapy it was still his nest, his home which provided him great stability just as our homes and families do in our everyday lives even when we are away from them.

If we listen to these right-brain stories, the deeper intelligence will tell us what is best for us in therapy and why. Communicative therapy is preferred by the deeper intelligence itself—as I have heard from hundreds of patients themselves—because it is the therapy which knows how to hear the remarkable voice of our deeper mind.

In this day and age when so-called "fair-minded thinking" often means everyone's ideas are equally valid, we must be very careful. That line of thought implies that no one can say one form of therapy (or anything else) is superior to another. Taken to the extreme, this "fair-minded" thinking eliminates the possibility of ultimate truth and can squelch breakthroughs.

THERAPY IN OUR CULTURE

Many people today are justifiably concerned that psychotherapy is receiving too much attention and that our culture as a whole has become too dominated by a therapy mentality. For example, critics note that many educators seem to be focusing on creating therapeutic environments instead of educating, and a feeling-centered subjectivity has sneaked into various curricula. Feelings are held to be the primary determinate for decision making, which means ultimately that logic and truth take a back seat. Without question, our understanding of the deeper intelligence shows that these criticisms are right on target.

The problem is that a mentality springing from an inaccurate therapy has been allowed to flourish. What we are seeing is a culture dominated by left-brain therapy when a right-brain therapy is far superior. Of course, many of these left-brain therapists (or those whose espouse left-brain values) will claim that they are truly right-brain therapists and address the deeper mind—since they seem to look at the deeper (hidden) issues. The fact of the matter is that most of these therapists are not dealing with the deeper mind at all because they ignore the deeper intelligence.

Along these same lines, certain people have become so concerned with the triteness and vagueness of psychological language, as well as the irresponsibility psychology often encourages (by leading patients to inappropriately blame their problems on others), that they refer to psychological explanations as psychobabble. Into this often chaotic picture of therapy, the language of the deeper intelligence is crystal clear in its descriptions of our deeper mind and the crucial issues facing all of us. The deeper intelligence itself clearly distinguishes what is psychobabble and what is wisdom to cherish from a brilliant mind far more capable than our conscious mind.

Perhaps the best way to understand the difference in psychobabble and deeper intelligence language is to see that the deeper intelligence gives us a way of "measuring the mind." In *Rating Your Psychotherapist,* Robert Langs described how he had studied the meaning (to a patient's right brain) of certain boundaries such as frequency of appointment times (once a week versus more irregular visits) or total confidentiality (even when a patient requested a third party be included in some way), and it quickly became apparent how the deeper intelligence was speaking clearly and rendering an opinion on each boundary. Thus, the deeper intelligence was able to communicate so definitively about the conditions it needed in therapy that Langs was able to define nine basic boundaries or ground rules of therapy.[4]

Perhaps the best way to understand the difference in psychobabble and deeper intelligence language is to see that the deeper intelligence gives us a way of "measuring the mind."

The breakthrough to the deeper intelligence offers an incredible unifying opportunity to our culture, because deep down, we all agree on the basic rules of life. Yet, as with any new discovery—exciting as the deeper intelligence may be—we must also be careful not to think it is the last word on the mind, which I see as humanity's last great frontier. In fact, the breakthrough to the deeper intelligence has been so shocking (to think that we all speak a hidden second language without recognizing it) it makes us realize many other possibilities may exist. Is it possible, for example, that another hidden language of the mind will be discovered? Or are there other abilities of our mind beyond our wildest imagination?

Whatever is discovered in the future, I am confident it will not violate the needs, standards, and values the deeper intelligence has put before us, because the values it affirms—individuality, integrity, and commitment— are universal. If as a culture we listen to this marvelous wisdom, it also will point the way to the prevention of many problems.

Finally, through the discovery of the deeper intelligence—which I believe is the most important break- through in the history of psychology—we can now see our Creator, the Architect of this amazing mental capacity, far more clearly than we ever have. When we consider that *psyche* means *soul*, the fit between psychology and relig- ion—between the mind of humans and their spiritual needs—ultimately is a perfect fit. Psychology can play a surprising role in leading the way to a healthy spirituality.

I believe fully understanding the deeper intelligence will bring us closer than ever before to the wonderful and terrifying face of God. But that is your judgment to make.

I believe fully understanding the deeper intelligence will bring us closer than ever before to the wonderful and terrifying face of God. But that is your judgment to make.

CHAPTER THIRTEEN

The Deeper Intelligence and Spirituality

"Man by the Fall fell at the same time from his state of
innocence and from his dominion over nature. Both of
these losses, however, can even in this life be in some
part repaired. The former by religion and faith, the
latter by arts and sciences."[1]

Francis Bacon

The short, compact, muscular man in his thirties
paced back and forth in the small room. Jordan was
agitated—and despite his efforts to express himself by
talking, he was so frustrated that he had to pace; words
alone were not enough to give him relief. Frequently he
berated the man who was sitting quietly listening to him,
his psychiatrist, Dr. Daniel Bird.

"What do you want me to say?" Jordan spurted. "I knew
this therapy wouldn't help me. What can you really do for
people? You're a doctor—what do you know about suffering? Look at you, sitting over there with your nice sport
coat on, in a fine office."

Seeing his patient's extreme agitation, Dr. Bird
thought, *I've been doing this twenty years, and I've seldom
seen a patient this afraid.* Jordan had to get up and pace
more than any patient he'd ever encountered.

Therapy had been stressful for Jordan, but until now he

had been able to tolerate it. Dr. Bird had considered using medication just to calm him down and keep him from being overwhelmed, but Jordan had already made it clear he would have no part of that. He also had been to a few other counselors and thought they had been of no benefit. Knowing Jordan was at a crucial moment, Dr. Bird thought, *If only he could face the pain which torments him, he could be free.*

Dr. Bird understood exactly what the fear was that Jordan had to face. His horrible past, which he had described in vivid detail the first two sessions, was haunting him. In a very tangible way, it was as alive today as it had been thirty years before.

Jordan was in the process of having to learn to trust and to accept that close relationships could be safe. He was learning this for the first time, after thirty-five years of believing the opposite. To do that, he was looking all of those hurtful experiences of the past in the face and attempting to "detoxify" them. (Jordan had to reexperience his damaging past experiences within the context of therapy, where he would come to fear his therapist. Jordan had developed the erroneous idea that in a one-to-one relationship he would always be destroyed, as he nearly had been earlier in his life. To be healed he had to learn first-hand that this idea was not always true, and that there were certain one-to-ones he could trust.)

Jordan had always avoided closeness, creating numerous escapes for himself, all designed to keep him at a safe distance from relationships and to obliterate his pain. Primarily he had settled for brief, uncommitted relationships or avoided them altogether. He also had tried to bury his problems in the temporary comfort of alcohol. The idea of trusting someone was to him a life-threatening risk he didn't think he could take.

The immediate crisis had come early in Jordan's therapy. At first he had talked about why he had come. He had lost control of his life and wasn't functioning well as a supervisor in a coal mine. He was single, unfulfilled, and without any close relationships.

Then he had talked about the troubles in his past, growing up watching his parents argue and fight. Several times he'd seen his father hit his mother. His mother eventually became an alcoholic, and Jordan was shipped from relative to relative and occasionally to a foster home.

Now, in psychotherapy, Jordan had increasingly talked of his distrust of others. Dr. Bird waited through another period of Jordan's berating him until finally his patient's punishing intelligence revealed itself. "I watched my father abuse my mother. I've seen people trapped and killed in the mines. I've had a hard life, and you're not making it any better."

These were the clues Dr. Bird had been waiting for. He quickly pointed out to Jordan that what really lay behind his trouble was that all private relationships—which he so desperately wanted—stirred up tremendous thoughts of people being hurt. Dr. Bird knew that Jordan didn't think he could trust anybody—even his therapist. In a painful way, Jordan expected he would be hurt in relationships today, just as he had been in the past.

Jordan replied, "You're right. I don't trust anyone, not even God. In school I tried to find a religion to believe in, but none of it made any sense to me. I wanted to believe, but somehow I just couldn't.

"Religion seems so fake. All this faith business. Look at the world and tell me God did a good job—all the hypocrisy and suffering. There are a lot of religious people talking about the judgment of God. Please! Give me a God of love, even though I don't think he exists. None of this business about judgment.

"I wish I could be like the new miner in my crew who has a lot of faith and is always optimistic. He hasn't been as frightened in the mines as most new miners are. He listens well, unlike some of the other people who work for me. A lot of those guys won't hold a job very long."

After hearing this, Dr. Bird attempted once more to show Jordan again that deep down he thought of close relationships as similar to being trapped in a mine. This fear caused him to run from one-to-ones. He pointed out, too, that another part of Jordan wanted to overcome this fear as he talked about how well someone else was doing when he overcame his fear. If Jordan didn't stick therapy out, Dr. Bird said, he would be like those miners who never learned to live in tight spaces; he would continue to have a lonely, meaningless existence.

Jordan listened for a while, but finally he announced he was going to stop therapy, which he did, never to return.

After Jordan's last session, Dr. Bird tried to think if there was anything he might have done to help this desperate man. Should he have tried just to "be a friend" to Jordan, to empathize with his pain? But Jordan had already had a therapy like that and often complained about its ineffectiveness. Dr. Bird wondered if he should have suggested medication, but Jordan would never have considered it. Would a consultation with another therapist have worked? But Jordan had had a hard enough time coming to see him.

Despite the grief Dr. Bird felt for Jordan, who could not face his pain in order to obtain healing, Dr. Bird concluded there was nothing else he could have done.

Dr. Bird knew that Jordan had been offered a chance at the healing his deeper intelligence wanted, but the pain was just too great for him. The therapist thought, *Perhaps down the road Jordan will remember the fact that another human being was willing to face his fear with him, and perhaps seek out therapy again. But Dr. Langs is right about these kind of patients. He calls them "the damned."*[2] *The very healing process they desperately need terrifies them. They need to be able to trust, yet they are overwhelmed by distrust.*

THE SPIRITUALITY FACTOR

Why is the subject of spirituality or faith so important in Jordan's story? And why might it be important in a book mainly discussing the mind? Aren't religion and psychiatry at odds with each other? Spirituality seems mystical and far removed from the realities of working out conflicts in our day-to-day relationships.

In one sense, the answers to these questions are simple. The deeper intelligence has broad influence because the way we gain and process information is important to every kind of relationship and endeavor. This applies to our spirituality as well.

In a remarkable statement made some two thousand years ago, the apostle Paul said that nature around us (particularly the nature of man) testifies to the existence of God.[3] Now, obviously, there are quite a number of very bright people who don't believe in God. So how could Paul make such a claim that men intuitively and instinctively know about God, as there were atheists then as well as now?

I believe the apostle, at least in part, was referring to a human being's deeper intelligence—that gifted part of us that is always evaluating our environment in a thousand deep and different ways. Paul was making the case that humans are phenomenally capable of perceiving exactly what reality is, in particular, perceiving what is going on between a person and God. Furthermore, Paul asserted that people "secret away" those issues we prefer not to deal with—most importantly, the prospect of our relationship with God.[4]

No doubt, the discovery of the rest of our extraordinary mind and its phenomenal abilities reveals as never before the greatness of human beings. The mind is what separates us from the rest of nature's beings. It is our distinguishing mark. Indeed, it is a logical step from seeing the greatness of our mind to perceiving the greatness of the mind of the Creator who made us, since we have been made "in His image."

No doubt, the discovery of the rest of our extraordinary mind and its phenomenal abilities reveals as never before the greatness of human beings.

The early scientists, as they learned about nature, described their learning process as "thinking God's thoughts after Him." Thus, when we examine our mind, we come the closest to seeing a reflection of God's mind—the closest to "thinking His thoughts after Him."

I am not suggesting, of course, that even with the deeper intelligence we know one-millionth of the thoughts of God. But the deeper intelligence is a wonderful starting point when it comes to grasping the greatness of God. As a friend of mine said when he began to understand the breakthrough to the deeper intelligence, "The deeper mind bears the thumbprint of God."

Yet, before I explore what the marvelous deeper intelligence itself sees in nature and the remarkable things it has to teach us about God, I want to address the issue of unbelief.

In the final analysis, we must recognize that there are basically only two choices of opinion regarding our origins: creation or evolution, pure coincidence or intentional planning, chance or dance.

The closer we look at our magnificent mind, the more we understand it simply could not have come into existence by chance. Our exquisitely sensitive, capable, magically computer-like mind had to have been crafted by a

Master Craftsman. To believe that the human mind developed by chance is to me, a lifelong student of the mind, to believe something a million times more improbable than a hurricane hitting a nuts-and-bolts factory and producing a Boeing 747.

After we look closer at what the deeper intelligence reveals about our nature, I think this conclusion will be almost undeniable. (I say "almost" because the human mind can deny almost anything, particularly because of fear. Some people are so afraid of God that they must deny His existence. The deeper intelligence teaches us that it is fear that fuels our unbelief, our denial of God's existence.)

NATURE AND GOD

With the breakthrough to the deeper intelligence, our powers of observation have been significantly multiplied. Since the Greek word for *soul* is *psyche* we now have what I might call a "souloscope." When we look clearly at the heart—or the soul—of a person, we see not only her human needs (and fears) but her spiritual needs (and fears).

Since the one-to-one relationship is the bedrock of all relationships, I believe that the unique one-to-one relationship a patient and doctor have in therapy provides a partial picture of God's relationship with humans. (By no means do I wish to imply that a therapist is or should be a god-figure to a patient. I only wish to use this particular one-to-one relationship—because I know it so well from experience—as an illustration of the dynamics that take place in a person's one-to-one relationship with God. I believe that as we look at the deepest issues in one-to-one relationships we have with each other, we also will see the deepest issues we have in our one-to-one relationship with God.)

What are some of the similarities in the patient-therapist

228

relationship that suggest this picture of the relationship between God and a human being?

First, a patient looks to his therapist to help enable the healing process. I believe that during the time a patient is in therapy, it is the single most important human relationship in his life, so far as emotional healing is concerned. By analogy, if he needed physical healing, a surgeon might be the most important relationship for him to have. Nonetheless, a patient is frequently unaware of the importance of the therapist to him and often denies his influence in his life. Even patients who appreciate their therapist are blind to how important their therapist is to them—much as kids are blind to their need for parents.

This private relationship between a therapist and a patient suggests a picture of man's relationship with God—a secret, ongoing, powerful one-to-one relationship which is often denied or ignored.

In short, the patient is blind to the most important relationship in his life. This private relationship between a therapist and a patient suggests a picture of man's relationship with God—a secret, ongoing, powerful one-to-one relationship which is often denied or ignored.

Second, the relationship between a patient and his therapist points to our unmistakable need for adherence to the code of life by which we want to live.

If it is true that people are made in the image of God, then our moral code as humans should reflect our Creator's code. That means the code we find in the deeper intelligence should have everything to do with God. In fact, if we find a moral code deep within ourselves, that should tell us that God exists. It also should tell us that nature is essentially moral. There's no reason to conclude that a chance universe would have a universal moral code.

The obvious question then becomes: Which code of behavior, if any, among the world's religions does the deeper intelligence's code point us toward? To answer that question we must examine what the deeper mind teaches us about our basic needs, which form the basis of the code of life we demand at our core. The themes of those needs are commitment, loyalty, fidelity, integrity, and freedom. I believe this code is most compatible with the Christian code, particularly with its emphasis on the accountability of the individual to conform to clear standards.

Upon close inspection, you'll notice that the natural code of the deeper intelligence and the revealed Christian code of life are the same. Both codes are enormously concerned with relationships. The Old and New Testaments of the Bible reveal that God is specifically concerned that boundaries in our relationships be clear, because boundaries give and protect life.[5] This explains why the Christian continually emphasizes not only grace but law—that is, where the boundaries go. This is the same emphasis the deeper intelligence places on boundaries.

It is important to note, however, that Christianity's emphasis on the law is not obsessive or punitive, as is commonly held; rather, we see in God's code an expression of His love and, thus, how He desires that we love one another. The first and foremost way we love someone is within proper, life-giving boundaries. Indeed, true love will never cease to be concerned about proper boundaries.

The deeper intelligence also sheds light on what we term sin—and it is clearly the same light that the Christian code reveals. Sin in both the Old and New Testaments is repeatedly referred to as *lawlessness*; it always has to do with breaking some type of law in relationships.[6] To put it another way, *sin always involves a violation of another person (including ourselves) within the context of a relationship.* This is precisely the definition of sin in psychotherapy, as patients who violate their basic needs or those of others are referred to as "frame breakers" or "destroyers of stability."

The deeper intelligence also sheds light on what we term sin.

Here we clearly see the punishing intelligence's link to sin. Because of its excessive fear of intimate relationships with clear boundaries, the punishing intelligence encourages us to live out compromised relationships outside of ideal boundaries, thereby sanctioning lawlessness or sin.

The punishing intelligence wants us to destroy life-giving boundaries, and the deeper intelligence wants us to honor them.

Ultimately, this fear which imprisons the punishing intelligence leads to self-abuse by encouraging us to violate the boundaries of others and allowing them to do the same to us. (Jordan, for example, had a long history of shallow and uncommitted, often hostile relationships, where he used others or they used him.) This illustrates the battle between the punishing intelligence and the deeper intelligence! The punishing intelligence wants us to destroy life-giving boundaries, and the deeper intelligence wants us to honor them.

ONE MORAL CODE FOR EVERYONE

The idea that there is one best code of life for every living person is not popular today. Our Western culture is pluralistic, and individual expression and freedom are highly valued. Many consciously reject the Christian code and thus the Christian God because it doesn't seem "right" to them that everyone should live by the same code. It just doesn't seem fair and limits the freedom of choice.

Some are terrified at the mention of absolutes. "Rigid" is their immediate view of those who advocate a consistent code of life for everyone. However, I believe that behind this conscious belief system that enshrines flexibility is an underlying fear of rules and enormous security anxiety. The prevalence of security anxiety explains why so many have willingly adopted the notion that everyone can live by a personal set of rules of their choosing.

The deeper intelligence without question shows that deep down we are all clearly in agreement with God that there is a universal value system. With the breakthrough to deeper levels of the human psyche, we discover that deep down we all want to live by natural laws, despite whatever differences we have over such laws in our conscious minds. In other words, we see that a natural law exists in the hearts of all humans, something the apostle Paul wrote about long ago.[7]

That deep down we all desire to live by a consistent code of ethics was also made clear by Robert Langs in his book *Rating Your Psychotherapist*, where he defines the consistent needs a patient has from a therapist. In laying out a set of rules for a therapist to go by, Langs revealed that people live by a set of natural rules or laws based on their deepest needs. In a nutshell, Langs found in psychotherapy that there were standards a therapist could go by and observe consistent effects. In every case, he found that the deeper intelligence consistently advises living by a definite standard, which is the same for everyone.[8]

When Langs discovered the rules of the mind in therapy, in essence, he discovered the rules of the mind outside of therapy. Therapy is only a part of nature. (Interestingly, in his later years Langs has begun referring to himself as a naturalist, so convinced is he that nature has a lot to say.)

As I have said, one major breakthrough often leads to other major breakthroughs. Thus, when we discovered the deeper intelligence we also discovered more evidence for natural law. (While many thinkers have contended for years that laws of human nature exist, this breakthrough in psychology provides the first "hard evidence" for natural law. By evidence I mean that Robert Langs established clear, consistent rules of the mind under the same "measurable" conditions (a patient in psychotherapy with definite boundaries), rules thus open to scientific validation. In other words, for the first time in history, the existence of natural law could be verified with solid research. I have no doubt such research will one day confirm that these laws of the mind exist (and already has to an extent), as many therapists along with Langs have witnessed unparalleled consistency in the ways of the mind.)

A brilliant colleague of mine, a fellow deeper intelligence-oriented therapist with an extensive background in philosophy, and also a conscious atheist, once remarked to me that the breakthrough to the deeper mind strongly established a universal moral code. As he put it, "this discovery [of the deeper intelligence] has incredible application to ethics." Though he wouldn't concede that this strongly pointed to a Giver of this code, his assessment was striking, given his theological views.

This confirmation of natural law will continue to be met with much resistance, for now we have a standard to which we must hold ourselves accountable. If we have learned one thing above all in working with the deeper intelligence, it's that human beings are terrified of accountability, however much they simultaneously cry out for life-giving boundaries. There are a number of people who prefer to live only by their conscious feelings, who insist that conscious feelings are the ground basis for truth instead of natural law.

But if, indeed, natural law exists, we have come to one of the great change points in history, not just in psychotherapy but in all of life. Scientists call these crucial moments "bifurcation moments," meaning we have come to a fork in the road and must choose which way to go. As a culture we can continue to deny that natural law exists, which is what has largely taken place in this century, or we can embrace natural law and begin to reap the advantages of living within the boundaries of that law.

We desperately need God's laws, but we are terrified of keeping them. Whether in psychotherapy or in everyday life, the very rules we desperately need to live by frequently frighten us and cause us to make unhealthy choices.

Thus, a code of life central to all humanity is not only

234

what the Christian code teaches, it is also what the deeper intelligence teaches as well. Furthermore, the deeper intelligence reveals that it is not that we disagree with the universal code but that we fear the very code that we know we need.

This takes us to the heart of our most basic conflict in life—our conflict with God. We desperately need God's laws, but we are terrified of keeping them. Whether in psychotherapy or in everyday life, the very rules we desperately need to live by frequently frighten us and cause us to make unhealthy choices—and, in the end, point us toward our relationship with God. This means our problem with God is different than we thought it was. One of the particular problems that humankind in this century has had with God—one code of behavior for everyone—has been solved by the deeper intelligence, which shows us that deep down we are actually in agreement with God. It's not that we disagree with God, it's that we fear God. (In the next few pages, I will also address another problem unique to our day and age, the ridiculing of faith.)

Parenthetically, I need to tell you why I believe the deeper intelligence knows God exists. If the deeper intelligence innately knows the rules of life, then it would only make sense that it also knows there has to be an Originator of these rules. An example that further confirms this is found in psychotherapy with children where youngsters are clearly and innately aware of these "rules of life," without having been taught them.

The deeper intelligence, brilliant as it is, understands that order and purpose come only from Someone with a purpose. Definite *values*—rules of human behavior—don't just evolve by chance; they are determined by a Ruler, a Creator. The deeper intelligence declares unequivocally that relativistic situation ethics are simply another way we lie to ourselves.

DOES THE DEEPER INTELLIGENCE SUPPLANT GOD?

At this point, some people of faith may fear that my emphasis on the greatness of our mind—the innate wisdom of the deeper intelligence and its efforts to guide us—undermines our need for God. Others may view the deeper mind as an entity in direct competition with God, who is to be the guiding light in our lives. Neither of these notions could be further from the truth.

Truth cannot contradict itself. If the deeper intelligence exists, then we would expect its "truth" to correspond to spiritual truth. And, indeed, instead of taking us away from God, the deeper intelligence brings us closer in a number of ways.

First, the deeper intelligence causes us to cry out to God because never before have we seen how blind we really are in our human relationships, particularly when it comes to seeing ourselves. When we begin to consider our significant limitations, then we are on the path to seeing God.

As we begin to grasp the extent of the blindness of our conscious minds, we become more curious about the extent of our spiritual blindness (a teaching central to the Christian faith). The fact that there is far more to ourselves and all of our relationships than we can immediately perceive leads us unmistakably to the distinct possibility there is much more about God and our relationship with Him that we don't immediately perceive.

As we begin to grasp just how frequently we block out important aspects in our human relationships, frequently creating distances in one-to-ones because of powerful emotional issues, we are on our way to considering that we do the very same thing with God. If we can't see ourselves or others very well (with our conscious minds), then how well do we think we will see God where the emotional issues are far more powerful?

As we slowly grow in our awareness of our capacity to deceive ourselves, we begin to comprehend that a terrible division—a "fall" from our ideal state—has occurred within us. It is precisely at such a moment of humility that we are open to considering that our conscious knowledge of God and His ways and desires may be severely erroneous and limited.

Thus there is a clear answer to those people of faith who ask: Is it possible for the deeper intelligence to operate apart from God or to try to usurp God because it sees truth so clearly? With the breakthrough to the deeper intelligence, we need God more than ever, for there is a major problem regarding the deeper intelligence. Many times in therapy, the deeper intelligence will be clearly attempting to guide the patient and will simultaneously present repeated thoughts of people who don't listen. At that moment the patient's deeper intelligence is telling them the truth about a particular situation and also telling them simultaneously that they are not going to be able to hear it. And they don't, as I have witnessed time and again. Strangely enough, at those times they cannot hear the truth or most of the truth they are telling themselves in their own words, just as Jordan couldn't.

Even psychiatrists familiar with the deeper intelligence tend to miss messages from a patient's deeper mind, particularly when they have failed a patient. Everyone struggles with hearing the deeper intelligence.

Nevertheless, I have witnessed significant psychological healing as a result of people hearing the deeper intelligence and living out its wisdom. But I am only talking about *partial* healing. I continue to see unresolved fear in patients lives, even after significant improvement. I believe the deeper psychological healing which we need can only come from resolving a primary conflict with God, because that's who we are ultimately afraid of.

To obtain the healing, however, we must get over our blindness—particularly our blindness when it comes to

God. We can't resolve a conflict with Him until we know He is there or, more accurately, until we quit denying He is there.

The deeper intelligence challenges us to deal with God as it continues to show us that there is a significant unresolved fear stemming from some source. Our fear is so great, so constant, that logically it could only come from one source. *This is the answer to why security anxiety is so pervasive, the question which has so puzzled clinicians.*

The excessive fear present in our primary relationships, and the soul's abiding belief in a consistent code of life, lead to the unmistakable conclusion that deep down we are interacting with God every second of our lives. Obviously, if God exists, this would be our most important and powerful relationship, and an ever-present one.

The excessive fear present in our primary relationships, and the soul's abiding belief in a consistent code of life, lead to the unmistakable conclusion that deep down we are interacting with God every second of our lives.

But here is where the deeper intelligence needs God's help. Without God's help we can't see God. For example, I am thinking of some very bright therapists who are familiar with the deeper intelligence but are blind to its implications for the spiritual life, blind to our most important relationship.

So we need God to see God and to see more of the truth ourselves. Just a smattering of this awareness forces us

238

into a position of extreme humility. Thus I believe the deeper intelligence is truly a gift from God, an agent of God designed to humble us as never before. And humility is a godsend, the main prerequisite for seeing God.

This is exactly what the Scriptures say, that despite the clarity of God's existence and of His moral code in nature, human beings still can not recognize it.[9]

The deeper intelligence reveals to us that even believers have a great deal to learn about themselves—often aided by therapy. Time and again in therapy I have seen people of faith who have a great difficulty hearing their deeper intelligence, too. In every case, not only is unrecognized fear a problem, but they also lack humility. When they walk away from their deeper intelligence, they walk away from resolving an issue, not only with another human being but deep down with God. All fears of God are not immediately resolved the minute someone becomes a believer in God. Believers must in a real way "work out [their] salvation,"[10] however certain the reality of their salvation is.

CONFLICT: PERSON TO PERSON, PERSON TO GOD

The deeper intelligence clarifies that at the deepest level of our minds, our primary one-to-one relationships are filled with the fear of judgment and destruction and with guilt (along with the fear of abandonment and death). These lead us to avoidance of one-to-ones and to make scapegoats of others. These are painful realities, and it is only our relationship with God that would explain why we live in so much fear and guilt in our human relationships, why we overread fear and guilt into every relationship. As I have said previously, the degree of security anxiety, or intimacy anxiety, is so great that we simply cannot explain it on the basis of childhood trauma, abuse, or even death anxiety. As much as any psychiatrist, Robert Langs appreciates how greatly an early experience in life can traumatize a person. Yet Langs himself continues to be puzzled by the extent of this fear in human beings.

Indeed, there is a "universal neurosis" of security or intimacy anxiety—and there is a reason why. We are constantly reacting to God—working out our relationship with Him—every moment of our lives, and this brings unresolved fear and guilt (in relation to God) into all our other relationships.

Why are people so afraid of God? Why so guilty? The deeper intelligence understands that humankind has violated the sacred rules of life and is guilty because of the tendency to violate the important boundaries of life. (Robert Langs calls us "natural law breakers.") The deeper intelligence believes in guilt because it believes in boundaries.

But why is our guilt so pervasive and deep? Here Sigmund Freud provides us a helpful and striking observation, one that ultimately points us toward a spiritual solution to our deepest problem. Freud observed a constant phenomenon in relationships: He called it the law of talion—what we might call the law of payback ("an eye for an eye"). If a wrong has been done, it must be punished. Justice, in other words, must be served. It is not in our nature to wink at hurts; we insist that the books must be balanced. The wrongdoer must somehow suffer equivalent to the suffering he has wrought. Deep down we require justice (and therefore punishment) to be balanced inside. We insist our imperfections be made right.

Robert Langs in his own way described the law of talion by showing how people who had violated the laws of nature in their relationships *unknowingly punished themselves afterward*—even when they didn't own up to what they'd done. The wrongdoers made decisions that caused them to suffer, becoming addicted to drugs, for example; gambling their fortune away; entering destructive relationships. As Langs phrased it, "You don't cheat nature."[11]

Thus, the law of talion in a way is an effort on our part to reset the life-giving boundaries that we require. We need rules because we desire to be as whole and complete as possible. We insist upon a certain type of perfection in our relationships; we want things to be made right, because we want wholeness.

An answer for the guilt which so haunts man, which leads to his fear and avoidance of God, is forgiveness. Yet the forgiveness we seek is not a cheap one but, rather, forgiveness based on the law of talion—the law of justice. Here the breakthrough to the deeper intelligence brings us to the point where psychology and religion meet. To enter the kind of life a person truly needs, he must deal with his guilt, and only a true atonement (or payment of the guilt debt) will effectively relieve it.

An answer for the guilt which so haunts man, which leads to his fear and avoidance of God, is forgiveness. Yet the forgiveness we seek is not a cheap one but, rather, forgiveness based on the law of talion—the law of justice.

We must understand in a new way why atonement is so important and why God can't simply "excuse" our imperfections as though they never occurred. Life must go on, and the law of talion and justice must be fulfilled, so that wholeness can once again take place.

Rarely has there been a clearer picture of our need for

atonement than in the film *Raging Bull,* which so fascinated movie critics that many voted it the outstanding film of the 1980s. A brutal film based on the life of boxer Jake LaMotta, it was filled with violence from beginning to end. Although LaMotta punished others, in the end he always punished himself far more than anyone else. LaMotta was most proud of his ability to take a punch and would frequently invite others to pummel him. LaMotta's self-abuse culminated in one of the most powerful scenes in movie history with LaMotta in tears alternatingly beating his hands and banging his head against the brick wall of a jail cell until he's senseless. This preoccupation with self-imposed violence begs for an answer to the question, "Why do people choose to suffer?"

At the very end of the movie, the director Martin Scorsese answered the question in a powerful but surprising way by closing the movie with a passage from the New Testament.

First the Pharisees question the recently healed blind man about his healer (Jesus) asking, "Is the man a sinner?" Thus, at the very end of this almost intolerably brutal movie designed to take us to the primitive heart of man, Scorsese suddenly makes reference to sin and blindness. Certainly Scorsese is using the Pharisees symbolically to represent humankind in general which means the question easily becomes "Is man a sinner?" In response to this fundamental question the blind man's answer is crystal clear—a healing has taken place, "Once I was blind and now I see." But the Pharisees, as always representing those who suffer because they can't see, continue in their blindness. (Yet the blind man sees only with the help of Christ.) Unknowingly, I believe, Scorsese's deeper intelligence was saying that people need to see that the reason they abuse themselves is because they are attempting to atone for sin—and to be free they need Christ to cure their blindness so they can see His atonement.

In my view, humankind cries out for a massive atonement—the atonement of Christ. When a person embraces Christ's death on the cross as "payment in full" for his deviations or sins, he makes personal the atonement he so desperately needs. As we look more clearly at the deeper intelligence, we see just how great our need for wholeness is and how greatly we need such an atonement to bring about that wholeness. Just as the patient needs a therapist to help him obtain temporary wholeness in his life, we need God in order to have permanent wholeness in this life, and in the world to come.

REVELATION AND FEAR

There is one last striking parallel between the patient-therapist relationship and a person's relationship with God. At the heart of the Christian revelation of God are the Scriptures, which have been (and continue to be) under great scrutiny. This book is not the place to try to make a case for the validity of these Scriptures (which I happen to think are substantiated in remarkable ways by proper analysis). Nevertheless, we must observe their importance.

As a therapist who has witnessed patients time after time retreat from the shocking observations of their deeper intelligence, I know firsthand the tendency to avoid powerful communication. I believe most of the criticism leveled at the scriptural record is based on just this kind of fear. Many discount the Bible's revelation because in that way they are able to avoid a true one-to-one relationship with God—the kind of relationship that demands we face up to our most frightening personal issues.

If as human beings we are all terrified of having a secure one-to-one relationship with a fellow human being, isn't it likely we would be a million times more reluctant to enter a one-to-one with an omniscient, all-powerful God? Yet, as is true in our relations with our fellow humans, once we enter a one-to-one relationship with God, we will experience infinite benefits. To do this—that is, to know God—we must read the Scriptures and let them speak to us. If we do this, we will see their power. Down through the ages people who have listened to the message of the Bible have told us of its power in their lives, its power to confront and yet comfort.

Part of psychotherapy's role is to reveal. At the right moment, the therapist reveals an understanding through language (a spoken word) so that the patient might resolve his hidden conflict. The Scriptures function in a comparable way. At their very core they offer us an interpretation, a revelation through a written word to help us resolve our basic conflict in our relationship with God. And getting over our fears of God and seeing His love is the essence of life that the one-to-one in therapy points us toward.

MORE INSIGHT TO COME

While this is certainly not the last word on man and God, I do believe that the area of spirituality is ultimately where we will see one of the most important applications of the deeper intelligence in the future. There are many therapists and counselors with strong spiritual commitments who, as of yet, are unfamiliar with the workings of the deeper intelligence. As they begin to listen to the deeper intelligence, while remaining in tune to the most basic psychological/spiritual issues at our core, I believe they will learn far more about how God Himself utilizes the deeper intelligence.

The deeper intelligence is an agent of God in the sense that it shows us more truth about ourselves and about God. Even believers can benefit greatly from their deeper intelligence as it has a deeper perceptiveness both about our human relationships and about our divine relationship. It shows us far more truth about ourselves and about

God than we ever imagined. It shows us how far we have to go to see ourselves, and then also to see God more clearly.

The deeper intelligence has provided a remarkable service to true faith. It has helped us to see how intricate a part of our lives faith is. It is a popular pastime today to ridicule anything having to do with faith, in particular to associate it with ignorance and blindness. Believers often are held up for scorn. But, the deeper intelligence casts an entirely different light on the matter of faith. It shows us how often our feelings are blind and how often we need faith—logical faith—to see the truth about ourselves.

In a number of situations illustrated in this book we have heard the clear voice of the deeper intelligence speak in direct opposition to a person's conscious feelings. In virtually every case, if individuals were to benefit from the wisdom of their deeper intelligence, they had to trust their deeper mind over their feelings. As we have plainly seen, it was never illogical for them to have faith in their deeper intelligence over their feelings, but in fact more logical. Yet it didn't seem logical for them despite the fact that their deeper intelligence was in touch with reality more than their conscious feelings.

The deeper intelligence has provided a remarkable service to true faith. It has helped us to see how intricate a part of our lives faith is.

This helps us understand that when it comes to spiritual things, putting our faith in God's knowledge instead of our feelings is a very logical thing to do. Thus, true faith broadens our perspective and puts us in touch with reality far more so than our immediate feelings.

We are all people of faith—believers and nonbelievers alike. It is simply a question of where you put your faith. In therapy, a patient must either put his faith in his conscious feelings or in his deeper intelligence. When it comes to believing in God, we must either put our faith in our conscious feelings (which may tell us God is not there) or in God's intelligence (to which the deeper intelligence points). For too long, people of faith have been considered foolish. Now the deeper intelligence in a real way has brought authentic religion into the twentieth century and established that true spirituality is at the heart of our being.

The deeper intelligence in a real way has brought authentic religion into the twentieth century and established that true spirituality is at the heart of our being.

CHAPTER FOURTEEN

Building Self-Esteem

The tall, thin, well-dressed brunette who could have passed for a model looked like anything but a criminal and certainly unlike anyone who was suffering from low self-esteem. But the truth was the young woman, Yvonne, did behave like a criminal at times—compulsively shoplifting. Her behavior was criminal enough that she had been before a judge and was on probation. She also repeatedly complained of low self-esteem.

As I listened to her story unfold in her very first session with me, the thought ran through my mind, *External appearances can surely fool you, more at some times than at others. And this is one of those times.*

So how was I going to help Yvonne? Was I going to advise her at the right moment that her shoplifting was self-destructive behavior? Was I going to serve merely as an extension of her defective conscience and frequently warn her about the consequences of her actions? Would I attempt to institute stringent controls, such as a budget to enhance self-control; or was I going to try to help her understand herself, hoping in some way such an approach would help? Which tactic would be best and why?

It seems strange that behaviors such as compulsive

spending and shoplifting have to do with fear, but such is the case. Fear—what clinicians call anxiety—is very pervasive, and it disguises itself in a thousand ways. Low self-esteem and shoplifting can both be signs of fear, which explains how they can both occur in someone like Yvonne.

I was certain that at some point in her therapy, Yvonne would create a dilemma, and she would use this issue to reveal what drove her self-destructive behavior. It happened after several weeks of therapy, when she arrived twenty-five minutes late for a fifty-minute appointment. She immediately announced, "Since traffic on the freeway caused me to be late, I'm assuming you'll only charge me for half of the appointment." This, of course, was contrary to our previous agreement, but I didn't quarrel. I encouraged her to keep talking, which she did.

Yvonne told me, "I have a very big project coming up at work, and how I handle it will greatly affect my future with this company." Her self-esteem had been improving and was directly related to the independence and responsibility she had been given at work. Yvonne then mentioned, "One of my coworkers, Frank, has been stealing supplies from the company and padding his expense account. Now he wants me to lie for him, if they ask me any questions. I don't think I should. He needs to pay his own way and needs to be loyal to the company. I'm trying to be honest and he should, too."

A little while later, Yvonne said, "A lot of customers aren't paying their bills, and the company's cash flow has been a problem."

Near the end of the session, Yvonne noted the bad weather outside. She said it reminded her of the day she was trapped in a car in a frightening flood after a nearby dam had overflowed. Then she mentioned how frightened she'd been the time she was nearly raped; two days later the man from whom she had escaped killed another coed on campus.

Yvonne's deeper intelligence was making it crystal clear

to me what was behind her stealing and her low self-esteem: She was terrified of living in the type of committed, mutually respectful relationship she desperately needed for self-control and self-esteem. Unconsciously, she linked stability with danger and avoided it like the plague, to her detriment. In a previous session she had told me about being sexually abused by her father at a young age. Thus, at a crucial time when she was learning to trust important people in her life, she had been tremendously hurt by her father, someone she was counting on to be the epitome of commitment and stability. Because of this horrible experience, Yvonne now attacked stability whenever she got near it—both because she feared it and because she was angry and hurt. In the end, she cheated others as she had been cheated.

When I pointed out to Yvonne this pattern of behavior in her life and how it was being replayed in her relationship with me, she didn't like it. Characteristically, she reacted with anger: "I don't care what else my mind is saying. The fact is, I got held up on the freeway and you want to charge me for something I didn't get." For the moment, Yvonne was more comfortable being a victim. Nevertheless, later in the same session she talked about a very sensitive coworker who had been a great help to her (indicating that deep down she appreciated what I had said).

It took Yvonne several sessions to understand that her deeper intelligence was revealing to her how she refused to be responsible—whether it was for her therapy session or for her inclination to steal things. Her deep-seated fear made it difficult for her to hear her own ideas.

WHAT IS SELF-ESTEEM?

Self-esteem is perhaps the thing we desire as much as anything in the world. It means to be of value, to be recognized, to be validated as a person. This is a cherished desire at the core of our being. Even when we base our ultimate self-acceptance on the fact we have been forgiven for our imperfections by those who love us (particularly God), self-esteem still has everything to do with being valued.

Yet, if we examine self-esteem closely, we see that it is not what we might think. The path to true self-esteem and to wholeness can be tricky. Very often we unknowingly undermine our self-esteem. Yvonne wanted to deny herself the independence that was giving her a great deal of self-esteem and to shift what should have been her responsibility onto me by excusing her from a financial commitment. She also wanted us to break our agreement with each other as patient and doctor.

If we examine self-esteem closely, we see that it is not what we might think.

In other words, Yvonne wanted to break the fundamental rules of life and for me to sanction her behavior. She wanted to break the law of autonomy or independence, the law of integrity, and the law of commitment, and her deeper intelligence was telling her what she was trying to do. She was acting like the coworker who stole and should be reprimanded, like the irresponsible customers who didn't pay their bills. In effect, Yvonne was proposing to do away with the very way of life that was enhancing her self-esteem. And, secretly, with this plan she was guaranteeing her self-esteem would remain low. (Almost always when self-esteem is low, we somehow are violating the fundamental rules of life and unconsciously seek relationships that encourage us to do so.) Usually, these violations serve to perpetuate earlier patterns and relationships where basic needs were violated. Many times low self-esteem means there are issues hidden from our conscious minds to which we have failed to come to terms.

When self-esteem is low, we somehow are violating the fundamental rules of life and unconsciously seek relationships that encourage us to do so.

Yvonne's tendency to violate her deepest needs unsurprisingly was being played out in her everyday life. Over and over she selected unhealthy men who ended up deceiving her, who couldn't make a commitment, and who manipulated and controlled her as she gave up her autonomy. For this arrangement, Yvonne eventually paid a high price in her self-esteem. Her blind spot was costly.

We might say Yvonne had a left-brain plan for self-esteem that wasn't working. She wanted loose sorts of relationships in which she could be dependent and irresponsible. Often the men in her life were superficially charming and initially gave her self-esteem brief lifts ("left-brain boosts"). But the common thread in all her relationships with men was that eventually they violated her deepest needs. For the immediate boost of flattery and attention, she ended up being used sexually and emotionally without receiving any genuine commitment from them.

Yvonne's modus operandi was the same in her financial

dealings. She wanted loose, poorly defined boundaries in which she didn't have to meet commitments. She wanted to possess things even when she didn't have the money, as her shoplifting reflected. Yvonne also had another plan for her life, a right brain plan which revealed the type of relationship she really needed. Now because of Yvonne's deeper intelligence, we can see clearly that she possessed two separate value systems—and, in her own words (ideas), which one was the healthiest.

THE PROBLEM WITH REASSURANCE OR "STROKING"

A common ploy we use to raise our self-esteem is reassurance, or at times known as "stroking" or "flattery." There is a place for reassurance in our everyday lives, but it is not as important as we think. In therapy, especially, reassurance is a vastly overrated left-brain plan. Reassurance is one of the most common mistakes therapists make, particularly with patients who complain of being worthless and of having low self-esteem. This is precisely why a therapist's efforts to treat the problem of low self-esteem can often fail and why the problem appears to be so persistent. Many times a therapist is attempting the wrong cure—addressing the left brain instead of the right.

Self-esteem flows from our right brain to our left brain as we live out the fundamental laws of life, which are designed to fulfill us. Too many therapists think self-esteem flows from the left brain to the right brain, thinking, "If I can just reassure this person enough, it will sink into his subconscious." This simply isn't true. (It is true that some patients describe *feeling* better by direct validation of their self-esteem by their therapists; but what these patients don't realize at the time is what is happening deep inside them. Often, these same patients never make the connection when future problems, such as depression and hopelessness, occur. This is because of the side effects of constant reassurance, which deep down damages their coping strength and individuality.)

Self-esteem flows from our right brain to our left brain as we live out the fundamental laws of life, which are designed to fulfill us. Too many therapists think self-esteem flows from the left brain to the right brain.

The same problem occurs in everyday life. "Loving" parents can be overly reassuring and actually violate a child's needs for independence. "Kind" employers can be puzzled by their employees' inefficiency and failure to produce. They can completely overlook the fact that as leaders they are undermining their employees' sense of responsibility by not allowing them to make any important decisions or by never providing them the accountability they require. People need to be verbally affirmed, but they also need something much more: They need to be entrusted with tasks that say to them, "I *believe* in you."

SOURCES OF SELF-ESTEEM

Because of our fundamental need for autonomy, this need is a primary place to assess the state of our self esteem. The deeper intelligence reveals that we all possess inordinate abilities. Armed with this information, we can come to appreciate a number of situations where we are making contributions. For example, a mother who doesn't work outside the home and "contribute to the family economically," nevertheless makes tremendous contributions by building into the family unit loyalty, stability, commitment, and freedom. The mother is a child's "first therapist," and if she does her job well, she can minimize the problems her child will have down the road.

The deeper intelligence reveals that we all possess inordinate abilities.

Another common place our autonomy—and thus our self-esteem—is violated is in the failure to allow self-expression. When a person is not allowed to voice his opinion, particularly when he or she disagrees with what is taking place, autonomy is violated. Then a person doesn't know what to do with their anger and has to express it in secret, destructive ways—such as Yvonne did. Within bounds, we must all have the privilege of self-expression, particularly voicing our frustrations.

Another place to look when self-esteem problems occur is to see if our needs for integrity or wholeness are being met. One area where we all can strive for excellence is in being people of integrity. When we do this, we reap the self-esteem Francis Bacon observed to be the fruit of integrity: "A good conscience is its own reward."

This is what happens to patients like Yvonne if they stick it out in psychotherapy. As they become truer to themselves and begin to live with more integrity in therapy, this behavior spills over into their outside life and, slowly, their self-esteem improves. Indeed, if we have integrity as a goal, then we are moving toward one of our three greatest needs, for deep down this is who we greatly desire to be.

Our last area to look at in assessing self-esteem is to evaluate the degree of committed relationships in our lives. For example, Yvonne's ongoing involvement in numerous uncommitted relationships was tearing her down. As she got over her fear and began to establish mutually committed relationships instead of mutually manipulative relationships, her self-esteem improved. Knowing our deepest needs, we can make sure there are people in our environments who are committed to us and we to them. Self-esteem comes when others demonstrate to us we are of value by the commitments they make to us.

Our three basic needs demand that something solid, something substantive, be in place if our self-esteem is to flourish. We need solid commitments from key people. We want people who stand solidly for the truth and deal with us in a straightforward way. And we want substantive tasks to accomplish. This is why reassurance is less powerful than a solid act of loyalty by someone who lets us express our autonomy. In therapy, for example, a patient demonstrates his autonomy by expressing his deeper intelligence and then living out the commitment which the deeper intelligence requests (such as Yvonne had to do).

We are exquisitely sensitive and vulnerable people. Many of us have been damaged by powerful experiences, and the toll on our self-esteem has been high. None of us has escaped some form of damage at the hands of others, or even at our own hands. To facilitate the repair process, we must know the rules of our minds. It is comforting to know, for instance, that many times our left brain lies to us; when we feel low self-esteem, this is only the tip of the iceberg and not the whole story. It always helps to know that deep down we all possess marvelous abilities.

Many times low self-esteem is not the real problem but merely a symptom telling us that "detoxification" of previous traumas including a failure to express our autonomy has not been completed. This is where psychotherapy comes in. One of the great privileges of working with the deeper intelligence is to see its power in identifying the deep pain in our lives and leading the way to healing. Virtually always, when people deal with the pain they've hidden from themselves, their problems with self-esteem take care of themselves.

THE SPIRITUAL DIMENSION AND SELF-ESTEEM

The rebuilding of our damaged self-esteem is never complete without dealing with ourselves as spiritual beings. Our deepest issues point toward our relationship with God. Until those conflicts are resolved, we will still fear our Creator, an experience certain to damage our self-esteem. On the other hand, to be validated and completely accepted by the most powerful Being or Personality in existence does remarkable things for our self-esteem. Embracing the atonement of Christ, as discussed earlier, is at the heart of this solution.

There is much more to having and maintaining self-esteem than meets the eye (or the left brain). With the breakthrough to the deeper intelligence, we suddenly have the potential for a one-thousand-fold increase in our self-esteem. To reap the benefits in self-esteem from our right brain, we must overcome our left brain and the self-defeating part of our right brain, the *punishing intelligence*, in order to find our true selves and express ourselves in the ways that meet our deepest needs.

THE CULTURE OF (FALSE) SELF-ESTEEM

There are many false ideas abounding on self-esteem, many of which are having an undue influence on our culture. One of the places we see the repercussions of a shallow understanding of self-esteem is among educators. A preoccupation with student's self-esteem is frequently the driving force in the shaping of various curricula, from elementary school through college. In his new book *House of Cards*, Robyn Dawes of Carnegie-Mellon University calls self-esteem "the holy grail of pop psychology." Dawes goes on to point out the lack of evidence connecting self-esteem and performance, all the while bemoaning the decline in the American educational system.[1]

From working with the deeper intelligence, we quickly learn that many educators have not understood the difference in left-brain, feeling-centered self-esteem and right-brain, principles-centered self-esteem. In so doing, they make the same mistake Yvonne was making. Initially, it felt good to her to behave in a way that eventually undermined her true self-esteem.

This occurs when educators cater to their students' left-brain feelings of self-esteem and ignore the students' deeper and more important right-brain needs for self-esteem. This is a major reason for the decline in student performance. The same problem goes on in a number of other places in our society where well-meaning people are missing out on exactly where it is that true self-esteem arises.

A few innovative educators have recently demonstrated where the answer to true self-esteem and enhanced performance lies. Georgia Tech officials made a dramatic change in their "Challenge" program designed for disadvantaged freshman minority students. Previously, the remedial program had helped the students' self-esteem but not their performance. When officials began treating the students as though they were unusually bright instead of deficient, their performance changed dramatically. In the end, the right-brain self-esteem resulting from enhanced performance, I can assure you, was greater than the left-brain self-esteem resulting from simple reassurance.[2]

Self-esteem is not a commodity we come to possess with a brief reassurance from someone else, however important this reassurance may seem at the time. Instead, self-esteem—true self-esteem—is a result of a gradual process, a diligent search, as we become people of character. To enhance our self-esteem, we must look at the basic rules of life and ask ourselves if we are in any way violating them. Only people of character ultimately have their deepest needs for self-esteem met. At the heart of that character is an ability to admit when we are wrong and, simultaneously, to accept forgiveness.

OVERCOMING LOW SELF-ESTEEM

When we suffer with low self-esteem, we have in our personal development come to the place where we consciously believe we are of little or no value. However much others have contributed to this opinion about ourselves (and indeed others can have powerful input into our lives), we can either perpetuate this negative identity of ourselves or find ways of repairing our defective sense of self. Without question there are solid ways to go about enhancing our self-esteem.

The deeper intelligence has shed enormous light on us, and one of the first things it teaches us about ourselves is that we all have a tendency to repeat self-defeating patterns of behavior, because we live under the illusion that it's safer (and more familiar) that way. In other words, low self-esteem at times can be perpetuated when we continue to put ourselves in situations designed to devalue us because of our issues with stability or intimacy anxiety.

258

Like Yvonne, we can be avoiding the very stability we need, and in the process undermining our three basic needs as well as our self-esteem.

But the deeper intelligence shows us the way out of this dilemma by giving us a clear plan for repairing defective self-esteem, which offers us incredible hope. As always, whatever situation we find ourselves in, the deeper intelligence leads us to listen to the basic rules of life.

The truth of the matter about self-esteem for all of us is that eventually our primary problem should be a struggle with managing high self-esteem rather than low self-esteem. This is simply because we have all been given remarkable abilities and a phenomenal mind, a mind that in many ways reflects the mind of God.

The truth of the matter about self-esteem for all of us is that eventually our primary problem should be a struggle with managing high self-esteem rather than low self-esteem.

EPILOGUE

I hope that through this book I have opened up a new world to you—the world of your remarkable deeper intelligence. In many ways, the rest of your life can be a journey of discovery about "the rest of your mind," and I wish you well along that path. To close now, I'll distill some reminders to you on how to benefit from the deeper intelligence in daily life:

1. *Know how your mind works.* Understand that our two-level mind is often divided within itself over a single issue.

2. *Understand that your words and actions frequently communicate on two levels—that they have both a direct and an indirect meaning.* Many times we are unaware of the second effect or meaning. This means we often must be more open to others' impressions of us, as they may be accurately responding to an indirect message.

3. *The primary prerequisites for knowing yourself are integrity and humility.* Be willing to consider how much you don't know.

4. *Understand the secret way to get to the guidance mode you possess in your deeper intelligence.* It almost always speaks indirectly, through stories, or in other seemingly unrelated comments. The Creator built this feature into your being, and therefore it's trustworthy.

5. *Listen for stories that you tell, particularly at key moments in your life.* Key moments include major decisions, major frustrations, crucial moments in

child or adolescent development. You can learn to develop a "feel" for this. Lean on your loved ones to hear you in this regard.

6. *Trust your deeper intelligence.* It will bring key stories back to your mind to give you a second or even third chance to hear them. Your deeper mind is constantly trying to help you.

7. *Be willing to consider at any time that any word or story you say or tell can apply to you personally.* Remember the "log in your eye" story Jesus told.

8. *Become aware of others who are unknowingly trying to teach you about yourself.* This may be a spouse, child, or friend.

9. *Become aware of others whose deeper intelligence may be in a guidance mode in your presence.* They may be trying to use you to learn about themselves.

10. *Before you tell someone what you think her deeper intelligence is saying, you must have her permission.* Part of having permission generally means you have a strong relationship with that person.

11. *Examine your behavior at key moments, particularly behavior you dislike.* Somewhere in your discomfort, your guidance mode may be trying to get your attention.

12. *Amid conflict with others or yourself, often the deeper intelligence presents a key idea that suggests the best way to begin solving the conflict.* For example, an individual or a couple having difficulty might talk about a situation in which someone needs expert outside help in an attempt to suggest to themselves to seek therapy. The key idea is often corrective, because one of the three fundamental laws by which we live is being violated.

13. *Develop an appreciation of the three basic laws we live by.* It's amazing how many times we violate these laws in relationships. An angry comment or command often carries powerful second-level mean-

ings. But appreciating our needs for commitment, autonomy, and integrity is one way of validating stories, whether yours or others. For example, recall the parents who gave their teenage son, Brad, too much freedom (by letting him join a band) and then corrected their mistake. They heard Brad tell two different stories—one reflecting the error and one reflecting the correction. By knowing the basic rules of life, the parents understood the meaning of each story. In this case, their son's need for commitment and control took precedence over his need for autonomy.

14. *Usually logic—thinking things out after you think you've heard your deeper mind—will confirm messages from the deeper intelligence.* This is true particularly if you keep in mind how easy it is for you to be wrong.

15. *Become a better listener by realizing that often another person can't tell you the whole story immediately but that their deeper intelligence wants to help him tell you "the rest of the story."* Learn to listen to people for longer periods without interrupting them. You can develop a sense of when people need to talk, and these are often the moments their deeper intelligence is working overtime.

16. *Learn to listen to your dreams—another way of accessing the deeper intelligence.* Although I have not focused extensively on dreams in this book, nevertheless a proper understanding of dreams can be of enormous benefit to self-understanding. I did touch on many of the principles for looking at dreams in the unique way that Robert Langs has developed called trigger decoding. He explores this in his book *Decoding Your Dreams*, which would be helpful to read. Langs has also developed other ways of using dreams to know ourselves, which I think will be another wave of the future.

17. *Don't be afraid of therapy if you need it.* Remember, when you go to therapy you take your deeper intelligence with you, and it wants to lead the therapy. Pick a therapist who is sensitive to the deeper intelligence. (If you need help in finding one, you can contact me by mail in care of the publisher, and I can try to make a referral.)

18. *Virtually all major conflicts in relationships are related to the difficultly in tolerating a one-to-one, which leads to distancing techniques.* The distance and alienation in relationships that disturbs us is very frequently something we seek to perpetuate. Behind the distancing lies fear.

19. *When all of the blame for a one-to-one relationship gone sour seems to fall almost entirely on one partner's shoulder, you should suspect that something is wrong.* Many times in relationships we play into one another's weak points more than we realize because of the hidden tendency to undermine the intimacy or stability that we want. It is a constant temptation to externalize problems in a relationship onto the other or unknowingly to encourage a particular negative role in another. Every close relationship will experience such pressure at moments. These are the times to take a closer look at oneself and not just at one's partner.

20. *No matter how bad a one-to-one relationship has become, it is virtually never too late to rescue the relationship.* That is, if at least one person is willing to make changes.

21. *Begin to grasp that moment-by-moment you are building into others.* Think about what your words and actions are building. Remember, you reap what you sow.

These are just a few of the lessons the deeper intelligence has to teach us about living. Become a seeker, and this will enable you to know much more about your own remarkable deeper mind and to see many more applications for everyday life.

My best wishes to you on the journey.

Andrew G. Hodges, M.D.
Birmingham, Alabama, 1994

NOTES

Chapter One

1. Robert Langs, *Unconscious Communication in Everyday Life* (New York: Jason Aronson, 1983).
   Take Charge of Your Emotional Life (New York: Henry Holt and Company, 1991).
   Decoding Your Dreams (New York: Henry Holt and Company, 1989).
   Rating Your Psychotherapist (New York: Henry Holt and Company, 1989).
   The Therapeutic Interaction (New York: Jason Aronson, 1976).
   The Listening Process (New York: Jason Aronson, 1978).
   The Therapeutic Environment (New York: Jason Aronson, 1979).
   The Supervisory Experience (New York: Jason Aronson, 1979).
   A Primer of Psychotherapy (New York: Gardner Press, 1988).
   The Technique of Psychoanalytic Psychotherapy, Volume 1 (New York: Jason Aronson, 1973).
2. Bernie S. Siegel, *Love, Medicine, and Miracles* (New York: Harper and Row, 1986), 47.
3. Ibid.
4. Gen. 1:26: "Then God said, 'Let Us make man in Our image, according to Our likeness; let them have dominion over . . . all the earth.'"

5. C. S. Lewis, *Mere Christianity* (New York: MacMillan, 1952.), 9.

6. George Will "Important Events Take Time to Recognize," *Birmingham Post-Herald* December 27, 1993: 7.

Chapter Two

1. Sigmund Freud, *The Interpretation of Dreams*, 1899. [Present Edition, New York: The Modern Library, 1978.]

2. Robert Langs, *The Technique of Psychoanalytic Psychotherapy* (New York: Jason Aronson, 1973).

3. Continuing Medical Education Seminar, Lenox Hill Hospital Psychotherapy Program, New York, 1985.

4. David L. Smith, "The Concept of Transference: Fact or Fantasy?" *Journal of Communicative Psychoanalysis and Psychotherapy*, 8: 99–103, 1994.
David L. Smith, *Hidden Conversations* (New York: Tavistock/Routledge, 1991).

5. Lewis Thomas, *The Medusa and the Snail* (Viking Penguin Inc., 1979).

6. Gary Smalley and John Trent, *The Language of Love* (Colorado Springs: Focus on the Family, 1988).

Chapter Three

1. Peter Kramer, *Listening to Prozac*, Viking Press, 1993.

2. Sharon Begley, "Beyond Prozac," *Newsweek*, February 7, 1994), 37–41.

3. Simon Grolnick, *The Work and Play of Winnicott* (New York: Jason Aronson, 1990), 144.

Chapter Four

1. Andrew G. Hodges, *Jesus: An Interview Across Time*, (New York: Bantam Books, 1988).

2. 2 Samuel 12:1–7.

3. Robert Langs, *The Listening Process,* (New York: Jason Aronson, 1978).

Chapter Seven

1. Ann Landers, "Dear Ann Landers," *The Birmingham Post-Herald*, January 19, 1994, 1E.

Chapter Eight

1. *The Birmingham News*, approximately 1987, Sports section.

Chapter Twelve

1. Scott Peck, *The Road Less Traveled* (New York: Simon & Schuster, 1978), 179.
2. Langs, *Rating Your Psychotherapist.*
3. Simon du Plock, "The Communicative Concept of Validation and the Definition of Science," *Journal of Communicative Psychoanalysis and Psychotherapy* (1992).
4. Langs, *Rating Your Psychotherapist,* 57–58.

Chapter Thirteen

1. Francis A. Schaeffer, *The Church at the End of the Twentieth Century* (Downer's Grove, IL: InterVarsity Press, 1971), 9.
2. International Society for Communicative Psychoanalysis and Psychotherapy Annual Meeting, San Francisco, October 1992.
3. Rom. 1:19–20.
4. Rom. 1:28.
5. Prov. 1:7–9, 3:1–2, 4:4–7.
6. 1 Jn. 3:4.
7. Rom. 2:14–15, 1:19–20,25.
8. Langs, *Rating Your Psychotherapist,* 57–58.
9. Rom. 1:19–20, 1:25, 2:14–15.

10. Phil 2:12
11. See endnote 2, Chapter 13.

Chapter Fourteen

1. John Leo, "When Psycho-nonsense Takes the Place of Reasoned Debate."
2. William Raspberry, "When You Expect More of Students, You Get More," *Birmingham News,* (July 6, 1994), 11A.

Epilogue

16. Langs, *Decoding Your Dreams.*

LaVergne, TN USA
06 May 2010
181799LV00004B/9/P